NEXT STOP
MARTYR: The Life
and Death of St. Patrick

Cahal Bradley

Cahal Bradley

DEDICATION

This book is dedicated to our great-great-grand parents Peter and Margaret Bradley. Our ancestors lived through and survived the Great Famine of Ireland as they moved their family to Belfast. Without their bravery, we would not be living the gift that is life with our beautiful families. It is because of them we have been blessed with the talents of Cahal and his brother Hugh, who produced their literary gems that now provide us with a glimpse into the history of Ireland and its people. To them we are forever grateful.

Conor Bradley and Mike McDermott

PREFACE

This book was written by my Grandfather, Cahal
Bradley, a historian with a passion for religion. He
dedicated many years to the research of Saint Patrick,
reading every piece ever written of and by the Patron
Saint of Ireland. Cahal has left no stone unturned in his
determination of learning all facts of Saint Patrick's
life. Details such as where he originated, who abducted
him, where he was taken to and how he died. These
facts have never been uncovered until now. The Author,
Cahal has written other literary gems, one notably titled
'Parishes of the North'. This book is a detailed
description of each Parish in the North of Ireland and
can be found in the Belfast Central Library. Cahal also
found beauty in the history of community; his novel
'Next Stop Heaven', set around 1890 depicts the lives
of those living within his own Parish of Holy Cross,
Ardoyne. This true love story portrays the lives of
families who lived in this area, inspired by his own
family and the trials and tribulations of which they
faced. Cahal was a natural poet, taking elements of
one's personal life and expressing the emotions
embedded within through his words. His collection of
poems was published 'Songs of a Commercial
Traveler' in 1931. His brother, Hugh Bradley, shared
Cahal's keen interest for literature. Hugh wrote what
was later titled 'Next Stop Romance', published by his

grandson Mike McDermott. Mike and I have joined together to launch all three books which are now part of the '*Next Stop* 'book series. *The Next Stop Martyr: The Life and Death of St. Patrick* manuscript, written sometime in the mid-1930s, was found among some old Bradley family relics by our cousin Stephen Bradley.

All three books are available in paperback and Kindle to purchase on Amazon. We hope you enjoy each book as we share our family heirlooms with you all.

Many thanks,

Conor Bradley and Mike McDermott.

Next Stop: Book Series:

Next Stop Heaven

Next Stop Romance

Next Stop MARTYR: The Life and Death of Saint Patrick

ACKNOWLEDGMENTS

Jaide Bradley
Caitlin Bradley
Lynn Bradley
Christine McDermott
Stephan Bradley
Holy Cross Church Ardoyne, Belfast

Cahal Bradley

Table of Contents

Cahal Bradley

The Forgotten Saint

Every Shamrock tells us of Saint Patrick. In emerald letters, his name is written across the Emerald Isle. His teaching is engraved in the hearts and minds of the children of Erin, and the stalwart sons of the Old Land are hailed throughout the world as "Paddies". As long as the Shamrock grows, he will be remembered and as long as an Irish heart may beat, shall be revered.

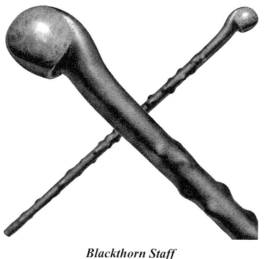

Blackthorn Staff

In mist and mystery much of his life and work lie hidden, but he comes so close to us we feel we can almost follow him.

Everywhere, throughout the Green Land, we hear his name. Everywhere, we hear his teaching. Hills that we see around us, still seem to ring with his prayers. Virtues, of bygone days, remain protected by his blessings.

Because of the charity he preached and practised, Ireland remains a land of hospitality. Because of his love of home, the exiled Irish feel their separation more. To aid the old across the hills, he gave to us the cherished Blackthorn, and to raise the young to golden dreams, he left his spirit in the Fairy-thorn.

Men, towns, mountains, and sacred wells carry his name, and the walls of the humble homes bear up his picture.

Today, Saint Patrick seems as near as when he walked

2

the five great roads of Erin, some fifteen hundred years ago.

To the history of the Saint there are two true guides. One is his own Confession, and the other his Epistle to the British Chieftain Coroticus. These are the two writings which the most critical of historians have accepted as having been originally composed by the saint himself, and all we know for certain regarding his work amongst the Irish, is gathered from them.

The confession was evidently written when the saint was a very old man – possibly immediately before his death. It is in Latin, and addressed to the Irish people, to whom he reviews his life, makes known his trails, defends himself against attacks and returns to Almighty God for all his mercies to him.

The other writing, also in Latin, was composed when he was about fifteen years younger, and is a letter of protest against the actions of the marauder called Coroticus, whose men had carried off a number of newly made converts.

Upon the testimony contained in both these treasured documents, we can, therefore, rely with confidence. Had they been lost, the name of Patrick might have been entirely forgotten, but, as if by a miracle, they were preserved, and today are universally accepted as being from genuine copies in the Saint's own hand.

Of course, there are several other writings which are said to have been the Saint's own, but, as much doubt has been expressed regarding them, I shall endeavour, with the aid of the Confession, the Epistle and helpful tradition to relate what is apparent of the life of Ireland's greatest Apostle.

That he was forgotten for a long time, a very long time is a painful truth. Why, it is difficult to explain; but, in a subsequent chapter, I shall endeavour to examine the cause and offer some attempts at explanation.

For over 200 years after his death, no life of the Saint was written, and his name had almost disappeared from Irish history.

To the Great Plague of 664-5, which decimated the monastic population of Ireland, and the Paschal controversy of the seventh century (concerning the correct date for observing Easter), we might attribute the destruction of a written life of the Saint, had we not the frank admission of his biographer Muirchu, when he was undertaking the task of recording Patrick, that he was, "launching the fail bark of his feeble intellect on a dangerous and deep sea, never, hitherto, explored or sailed upon by any ship." While seventh century Irish Bishop Tirechan makes it perfectly clear when he writes his "Life of a Saint", that the Abbots were remiss in their duty.

Saint Patrick, we learn, had died in the year 461, yet it

was not until about the year 700 the Irish writers began to awaken to the necessity of leaving a record of the great saint's life and work, for future generations.

By this delay so much valuable information regarding the Patron Saint of Ireland was lost, that as a consequence, even the earliest historians were forced to grope, as it were, in the dark.

The saintly National Apostle, who had laboured so long and with such self-sacrifice, passed to his reward, and sad to relate, was almost forgotten. Not one of the many learned companions, with whom he had worked throughout his life, has left us a written souvenir of the Saintly leader. None of the thousands whom he baptised made known his work. Truly, it is a sad admission. Few Saints were thus neglected.

Even the British scholar and historian Venerable Bede, to whom the records of the early Irish Church must have been available, and who lived between the years of 672 – 735 never mentioned Saint Patrick in his Martyrology. Ireland's silence in regard to the Saint must have, surely, led to this. Had Ireland been honouring him in those years, the Venerable Bede would hardly have omitted his name from his writings.

In the seventh century, when the Irish monk and scholar Cogitosus undertook the writings of the Life of Saint Brigid, it is most remarkable that he, also, never mentioned Saint Patrick. Even much earlier than this and closer to the time of the Saint's death, one is astounded at the neglectful silence of Ireland in regard to him. What was the cause?

Saint Columbanus, the great Irish missionary, who was born some fifty years after our Saint's death, has nothing at all to say about him, and the three great Bishops, Laurentius and Justus, who came to Britain about 100 years after his death, appear to have been unaware of his existence. Why, even the Christian writer and disciple of Augustine of Hippo, Prosper of Aquitaine, who lived in the days of the Saint, and, who recorded the coming of one Palladius of Gaul to Ireland, in 431, did not make any reference, whatever, to Patrick.

In Jonas's Life of Saint Columbanus, we find a similar omission, and when we come to Adamnan of Iona we discover that, except for a kind of the afterthought in his second preface, he has no further allusion to make to Ireland's Apostle.

Saint Patrick, it is quite evident, was for a long time mysteriously overlooked, and the lives of other Irish Saints written before his was ever thought of. Even his grave was neglected.

On glancing through the very earliest records, one is convinced the Irish hagiography has been regarded by the Irish monk and scholar Cogitosus (c 650) and, also during that same period, by the saintly biographer

Cuimine as beginning with the lives of Saint Brigid and Saint Columcille.

To us, it seems strange, however, that our Saint should have been thus shrouded so effectively in silence and that the writing of his Life should have been so long delayed. This must have some explanation. Let us in the meantime see how some of the memories of the other saints were treated.

Within a century after she had died, the Life of Saint Ita was written.

About a hundred years after Saint Brigid passed away Cogitosus had her Life and Work recorded. Friends of Saint Patrick may have forgotten him, but Constantius (c 480) left us a record of his companion and friend, St. Germanus; while Cuimine, wrote of Saint Columba about fifty years after the Saint was in his grave.

Considering these, and many other such illustrations, it is therefore, somewhat surprising to find that no Life of Saint Patrick was written until over two hundred years had passed, and we are disposed to add to the conclusion arrived at by Bishop Tirechan that the Nation, as well as "the Abbots," was remiss in its duty to the memory of its greatest Bishop and Saint.

The remissness, I fear, is not the full explanation for Saint Patrick having been forgotten for hundreds of years, and we shall endeavour to enquire further in another chapter.

He died… his name was almost unknown… his work… forgotten. Years passed. Then, towards the end of the Seventh Century, a Miracle happened, -- Ireland remembered Saint Patrick, and, in its remembering, one suspects the influence of those Saintly priests from Gaul.

The two first Clerics to give attention to the recording of his Acts, were 7th century bishops; Ultan of Ard-m Brecain, in Meath, and Aed of Sletty, in the present Leix.

Bishop Tirechan, under the guidance of the former, began his work shortly before the year 700. Whilst seventh century Leinster monk Muirchu Maccu Machtheni, acting under the instructions of the latter, had just completed, what he claimed to be, the first formal biography of Ireland's Saint.

As Saint Patrick is generally believed to have died in the year 461, we can see that even Muirchu's Life, which is believed to have been the first, was not written until over 200 years after the Saint had died. We might well ask, was this prolonged neglect deliberate? Was the slave-Bishop or foreign Saint not welcome to the nobles that succeeded him?

By the reader, it will be observed that both these Lives had their places of origin in South Central Ireland where "Saintly and learned men from Gaul frequented" and this fact, no doubt, caused several historians to conclude that our Saint only worked in that part of the country.

With these two interesting 'works' the 'Story of Saint Patrick' began to be followed and added to by each succeeding generation, until many Lives of the Saint have been so confused, and I might say so impossible, that it is not to be wondered at, that several able writers have denied his existence altogether, while others assert that he came to Ireland hundreds of years before the time that is generally accepted.

Immediately following the appearance of Tirechan's and Muirchu's works. Ireland seems to have awakened to its sense of duty towards the memory of Saint Patrick, and, with their arrival, innumerable references to the Saint are to be found in various historic records of the late seventh and early eighth centuries.

Ireland, then, began her devotion to Saint Patrick in earnest, a devotion that has not been dimmed by the passing of twelve hundred years.

Children began to bear his name. Hills that heard his prayers were discovered. Blackthorns resembling his staff were treasured. Holy thorns are considered sacred. Places where his blessed feet had trod were named after him, as were all the holy wells in which he had baptised his converts.

With fervour, the people of Ireland began to pray to him, and his spirit came to envelop the sea-grit land he had served and saved. It was, as it were, his resurrection.

Let us see what had been happening or what where the customs elsewhere about this time. In the Christian parts of Europe, we are told, at the time of the introduction of the Faith into Ireland, the custom whereby each community gave religious honour to its Martyrs, early Bishops and those eminent for sanctity, was well in practice. Already the deceased founder of each Monastery was held in special veneration.

Alas! How many monasteries must have been founded by our Saint in Ireland, yet he was not honoured. It is, therefore, some consolation to discover that a few learned historians believe that this custom, of giving religious honour to such men, did not pass to Ireland until the eighth century, which gives support to the belief that influence and concern from Gallic admirers of the Saint's work had something to do with the recording of his Acts in Ireland. In Gaul, at least, he had not been forgotten. It was, then, that relics of the Saint assumed much prominence and his book, his bell, his staff etc., became sacred. In this development it is convincing to discover that the first mention of a Maer (steward devoted to Patrick) appears under the date 814 in the Annals. By that time, and with surprising rapidity, the name of Saint Patrick had, at last, become honoured throughout the county and his relics "were being borne in reverence". Shortly before that date the Patrick Tribute, known as Patrick's Pence, has also been organised, and the Maer, referred to in the Annals, was the name given to each permanent steward appointed to collect this Tribute.

Already, at the request of the Primate Torbach (in the year 807) an official edition of the memoranda of Saint Patrick, now known as The Book of Armagh, had been prepared by the scribe named Ferdomnach.

Ireland had awakened. The name of the Saint was then kept in honour in the diptychs of the Church, and from entries in the Annals we discover that some records of him and his disciples were preserved in the Calendars and Paschal Tables, while in a Colophon to the Book of Durrow his name was invoked. But, although no Life of our National Apostle has been written for over two hundred years after his death, and his name seems to have been entirely neglected even by his companions, his memory had lived in the hearts and in the prayers that fell from the lips of the simple people.

With the growing interest, tradition was aroused and stories of Saint Patrick's doings became numerous, and the name of Quadrige (later Cothraige) or similar form, by which Saint Patrick may have been known to his contemporaries, was regarded and the Patricius of the Latin documents he had left was Hibernicised to

Patraic. A new Patrick was made but some of the old clothes the Saint had worn were still discernible.

The stories that we have been given by the earliest writers naturally show some confusion between the old "Q" name, the Patricius, and the earlier name of Palladius, but, written such a long time after the death of the Saint, we can readily understand this; and we suspect he was made subservient to what would be interesting and suitable reading, for an early writer tells he approached his undertaking, "with little skill, gathering material from uncertain authors, with frail memory, with obliterated meaning and barbarous language".

Thus, was an effort made to steal some light from the mist and mystery of two hundred years, and we know with what result.

The Capture of a Slave

In the year 405 the securing and selling of slaves was a common practice with most peoples. Strong young boys were then in great demand and fetched a good price. They were also "easy cargo" for a raiding party.

Flocks had to be cared for. Chieftains to be attended. Dogs required handling. Curraghs needed repairs. Firewood had to be gathered and fires kept burning. For these and similar occupations young lads were considered invaluable.

In Ireland each of the many tribes had its herds and hounds, while the warriors and clans of the coastline had their thousands of curraghs.

By the Chieftains of the inland parts many slaves were bought, and these were mostly supplied by the men around the coast, who stole them from other countries. Led by the most daring warriors, these Irish coast men frequently made excursions to other lands for the purpose of bringing back such servants, and even in those days, the law of supply and demand operated.

In the year in question, 405, Ireland probably had a good spring and a good summer, so, many workers being needed, the slave-snatchers organised an exceptionally large expedition in order to meet the demand.

Often such Irish missions had visited Scotland and Britain and had even ventured as far as the Continent.

The Great Roman Empire had begun to show signs of decay in the year 400, and, with its weakening, the Irish chieftains had grown more daring.

Already they had been priding themselves upon having contributed to its downfall by their persistent efforts on the Scottish front, for they hated Rome. Some, indeed, must have proclaimed that the fear of the strong arms of Ireland had prevented the Roman legions from ever entering their country. Some of the more ambitious spirits, were indeed endeavouring, as it were, to establish an "Irish Empire".

Against the powerful Romans the Irish and Scotch, having been in alliance, were on friendly terms so that, in the year 405, a raid upon Scotland for the purpose of obtaining slaves was entirely out of the question.

As regards to Britain, we are informed by reliable authorities that there is no record whatsoever of any such descent on that country in 405 or thereabouts.

That the boy Patrick was carried into Ireland by our chieftains, we do know from his own statement, but, as he did not make it too clear from whence he was taken, there are many different opinions expressed as to his place of birth and captivity.

Because, in his confession, the Saint informs us that he was taken captive "with so many thousand men" most writers have presumed it to have been impossible for such a heavily-laden expedition to have travelled far, and, are thus influenced to decide upon the nearest country to Ireland – Scotland – as being the place of his capture. Yet, in contrast with such a conclusion, we have the words of the Saint himself, written, mark you, when he was old, and knew both countries well, which states: "And the Lord brought down upon us with the anger of his Spirit and dispersed us among many nations even to the extremity of the earth". From this it is quite clear that some of the large consignments of slaves were distributed enroute at other countries, probably in South Britain and Wales, and as Scotch warriors must have assisted their Irish friends on the great invasion, they also, would have had their quota of the spoils to take home with them.

In this expedition, it would seem most likely that the Scotch had enthusiastically joined with their allies, thus accounting for its ability to bring back such large numbers.

Many writers having assumed the Saint was stolen from Scotland, and as the Saint himself seems to convey in his writings, that he never returned home after taking up his ministry in Ireland, it is further assumed, by them, that he never visited Scotland.

Palladius had visited Scotland, but concluding on this line of reasoning, that Patrick did not – we are therefore told that Palladius was not Patrick. But we shall leave this question to a later chapter.

Other historians have informed us that he was born and captured in Britain.

Even to a boy from Britain, Ireland could hardly have been considered "the extremity of the earth", and in respect to Scotland a similar mistake arises I t is presumed that the Saint never visited there, whereas tradition points very strongly to him having visited both of these countries and in support of this, we have the Saint's own statements. One in his Epistle which says: "I have vowed to my God to teach the nations" and another in his Confession where he refers to "those nations among whom I dwell".

Once having decided that the place of Saint Patrick's capture was either Scotland or Britain it became necessary to endeavour to fit these decisions to some of the Saint's own statements. In his Confession he tells us he was captured at Bonnavem Taberniae. The latter word conveys a Roman station, so a convenient one had to be found. Near the town of Dumbarton there had been such a place, so by those who favoured Scotland, it was pounced upon. Another such station had been in Wales, which is also near Ireland, so it was adopted, and every effort made to make both fit in to the name Bonnavem, without taking into account that fact that all the Roman Stations of Scotland were deserted in the year 405 and that the name for such a station in Wales was Castra (Chester).

When we read the hundreds of lives that have been written of Saint Patrick, we are amazed at the number of places where he is said to have been born.

It has been asserted that no less than seven cities contended for the honour of being the birthplace of

Homer, the Prince of Poets. To Saint Patrick as many countries have made their claim.

Because he said in his Epistle: "to them it is a disgrace that we have been born in Ireland," some have proclaimed him Irish. Because of certain descriptions he has given in his Confession, some have acclaimed him Welsh. Because of the size of the Irish seizure many have concluded he was Scotch. In the year 1187 the Monks of Furness Abbey insisted he was British. A number of Continental writers tried to prove him Italian. An old Life, because of a misunderstanding of some of his words, states he was a Jew and, various writers endeavour to prove that he came from various parts of Gaul.

Writing in Ireland when his life's labours were nearing an end, the Saint himself, always, definitely, declared that his native country was far away. Even to an old man in those days, and an old man of such greatness, Scotland, Wales, or England would have hardly been considered thus, nor, if he had come from any of these countries, could he have written: - "I am a servant in Christ to a foreign Nation, in the uttermost parts of the Earth".

Even in his expressions regarding home and his people, one can almost measure the distance of his separation.

For the place of the Saint's birth and capture we must, therefore, go much further than to Scotland or Britain, and of the many places suggested, we see no reason to doubt the very first record by the poet and chief bishop of Leinster, Saint Fiacc (c. 415-520) himself, viz: Nemthur, and this we take to mean Holy Tours in Gaul. Holy it was, then made holy by Saint Martin.

The Gallic-Roman settlement of Tours is situated on the Loire, and in those neighborhoods the friends and family of Saint Patrick resided. At the time that he was interrupted in his play and dragged from his homeland, the boy Patrick was little more than 15 years old, and the arrival of the huge army of Irish marauders must have been, to him, a terrible experience.

Disturbances there were, and plenty, in his own country, but the influence of his father and his noble birth, may have, frequently saved the lad from molestation. Not so on this occasion.

Where his parents were at the time, we do not know, but the boy, probably attracted by the great activity on the blue waters of the river, which ran close by his home, exposed himself to danger, and then realising it, ran in terror to the house. Here he possibly was followed and captured, as he says himself: "they took me captive and laid waste the servants and handmaidens of my father's house".

From these few tragic words, we can form some idea of the awful destruction that was wrought by this band of Irish Invaders.

Then Saint Patrick tells us, he "was taken to Ireland in captivity". To the quiet green hillside of Ulster, he was dragged from the bloodstained banks of Loire. Of noble birth, his father, Calpornius, was a decurion, a Senator and tax collector of the Roman Empire, so the boy was a member of the ruling class, a patrician, thus his name.

He "was nearly sixteen years of age", he says, when this wild Irish horde surged into Holy Tours, slaying and plundering and carrying off their booty and captives. What destruction must have been befallen the home and servants of the proud decurion! What indignation he must have expressed on returning to find his young son carried off, his residence destroyed and plundered! No wonder that throughout his life he never could have forgiven the Irish people, and even pleaded with his son not to go to them as a bishop.

Indeed, from the Saint's writings, it would appear the indignant father looked upon his son as a fool, for accepting such a mission. The marauders knew what they were doing. They had penetrated far into the country, scattering along the riverbank they made Tours their objective, and visited the places best provided with the kind of plunder they were in search of. These were the boot-leggers of the fifth century, and wine from Gaul was ever welcome in Ireland.

Gaul had previously been found a profitable place to visit. The Irish knew it and the natives feared them.

Only a few years previously Saint Jerome (342? – 420) in his Adversus Jovinianum, had testified to having seen these Irish warriors in action in that country, and wrote of the terror they caused. With the decay of Rome, they appeared more formidable. To Gaul they were not strangers, and their curraghs were often seen coming up the River Loire in large numbers, and on different missions.

River Loire

On this occasion, one slave was taken after another, but men and boys were apparently specially sought for, as the Saint himself makes know of "men" only. Hundreds of the warriors watched the boats in the river while the others carried out their wild raiding and slaying. Every prisoner was made to carry something. Roughly dragged or driven with the others, the boy Patrick had to shoulder his share, and carry his load to the curraghs that lined the riverbank. Into them the captives were then bundled and made to help with the oars or cargo, as the Irish fleet put off bearing young Patrick and his fellow country men into slavery. With tears in his eyes, the poor lad must have watched the hills above his home fade from his sight. Sobs were stifled and no cries uttered, for the stolen ones knew too well how near they were to death in company with such men.

On a hillside where Patrick's tearful eyes may have rested is seen, today, a kind of blackthorn bush which blooms at Christmas time and is known by the name of "The Flowers of Saint Patrick" and which is not unlike the Holy Thorn of Glastonbury, where the Saint in later years had been. At a short distance, along the same riverbank where the young slave was dragged, we find the picturesque little town of Saint Patrice. In that part of Gaul, at least, our Saint has not been forgotten. The river Loire along which the Irish fleet of curraghs had travelled, was well known to the raiders. Irish seaman of consequence had visited it. From the most ancient times trading had been carried on between Ireland and the West Coast of France. The mouths of the Loire and Garonne Rivers had become the popular destination for Irish traders. Wine, which was largely used by the Irish, was the most important article of commerce. Ireland could not produce it, and thus this route was very ancient, going back to the bronze and Neolithic ages.

It is not difficult to understand, therefore, why Gaul became the Irish equivalent name for foreigner, and also why in later years, the boy Patrick, referred to Ireland as a "foreign nation".

For centuries continual intercourse had existed between Ireland and Gaul. Into the mouth of both rivers in question, boats from Ireland often came, bearing cargoes of Irish hounds, which were in great demand on the Continent, and these boats returned with wine.

Others were invading Gaul in this year, so the Irish had also paid it a visit. It was a time of invasions. Roman civilisation was tottering. Everyone wanted a share of the spoils. And so, the expedition from Ireland and Scotland was both strong and bold. Its many curraghs were packed with plunder, as it sailed up the Loire, and made out to sea. Some of this enormous fleet may have stopped at the Cornish Coast, to dispose of their capture, others of it may have proceeded to Scotland, but we know that the main part of the expedition came on to Ireland, and carried with it the slave-boy Patrick, who "daily used to feed the cattle".

The Pagan Slave-boy Converted

Some writers have stated, that when the boy Patrick was carried into Ireland and sold to Miliucc, the country was entirely a pagan country.

Ireland, however, even at that time, 405 AD was not without some Christians.

The brutal raids of the marauding chieftains into other countries, had unknown to themselves, carried back the

Faith. Young girls, who had been reared in Christian homes, had already in their serfdom, grown to Christian womanhood. Young boyish eyes that wept on being dragged from their Christian parents, had grown dim and old with looking towards the heavens, from the Irish hillsides. The slave-boy and the slave-girl, who were Christian, became the more fervent in their exile and their slavery. Many of these were in the country. Even some of the pagan chieftains had Christian wives.

The boy Patrick was not long engaged in minding his cattle in County Antrim, when he came in contact with young slave-boys who were Christians. Serfs and chieftains did not mingle, but serfs and serfs did, and so the boy from Gaul soon found friends amongst those, who like himself attended cattle in the fields. Patrick grew fond of these boys. Possibly some were from his own country and could talk to him in his own language. Often, as they sat on the quiet hillsides, keeping a watch over their herds, he may have heard stories of their capture and slavery, and often told his own.

To the members of the Irish lower social order, the slave was always an object of pity. Many pitied him and some were kind. Patrick soon learned the language of the country, but in his slavery, he received a greater gift – the gift of Faith.

To Ireland he had come a pagan, and in Ireland he received the Faith. There is no misunderstanding the

Saint's own words: "I did not know the true God", he says, and again speaking of his captivity in Ireland, he avows, "And there the lord opened to me the sense of my unbelief." Ireland gave to him, with its punishment, the priceless gift of Faith. Here he discovered, apparently for the first time, the magnitude of a sin he had committed a short year before he had been taken into captivity. "I was taken captive," he tells us, "Before I knew what I ought to seek, of what I ought to aim at, or what I ought to avoid." But he was not long in charge of cattle in Ireland, until he learned to pray night and day and when he afterwards escaped from his exacting master, he left the island realizing, "what to seek, what to aim at and what to avoid." Here he awoke to the love of his Heavenly Master and atoned for his sins upon to Irish hillsides. Praying often and fasting often, he burned with the love of God and in later years, did not forget the faith he had found in Ireland, for in joy and gratitude he exclaimed, "Wherefore, I cannot keep silent concerning such great benefits and such great favour as the Lord had vouchsafed to me in the land of my captivity." Ireland saved the boy Patrick, and the man Patrick returned to save Ireland.

Whether he remained longer than six years as a slave in Ireland, we do not know, but we are aware that he served the druid, Miliucc, for that period.

Miliucc lived in the present County Antrim, and Silua Uluti (the wood of Ulaid), of which we are reminded by

Killyleagh, east of Lough Neagh, is a place where the shepherd boy once watched over his flocks.

The druid Miliucc was also a King and needed many servants. To him the boy Patrick, as he grew older, also grew more useful. The king's men also found him of service.

Often the boy with others drove cattle to and from distant places. On the roads the poorer people were kind to him. They sympathised with the noble lad in his position, as they pictured one of their own children a slave. They gave him food and gave him affection. As he became familiar with the language of the people he could converse with them, and he heard the wonderful stories of ancient Erin. Possibly, he often drove his cattle into County Down and there saw the boats come sailing into Strangford Lough and thought of freedom. He may have met and chatted with the boatmen and asked them if they ever went to far-off Gaul – his homeland. Gradually he became familiar with the manner of life of the people and grew to love his fellow slaves. Then as he increased in years, he longed to set them free.

Looking down from the Mountain of the Moon – that strange, shaped hill of Slemish, how often must the princely lad have fervently prayed that he might be free? And it is not unreasonable to assume, that by the kindly people whom he met, he was often encouraged to escape.

For six long years he served Miliucc, during which time, he tells us he "prayed frequently" and that "the Love of God and fear of him, increased more and more" until eventually he "used to rise to prayer through snows, through frost, through rain, and felt no harm."

Then at last, one night, as he slept, he heard a voice whispering in his ear, "thou shalt go back to thy own country, behold thy ship is ready." What joyous news to the little herdsman! What a consolation was contained in the promise to get back home! For freedom he had daily, aye, hourly, prayed, and now it was being offered to him. God had answered his prayers.

Making ready for the journey, he tells us that "after a while" he "took flight and left the man he had served for six years." Wandering through fields, in the darkness of the nights, and avoiding the great road, lest he should be discovered and dragged back to his master, the fleeing lad journeyed, he tells us, "Perhaps two hundred miles," until he reached the port from which the ship to bear him out of the country was sailing.

In his writings, the Saint himself makes known that he escaped from Miliucc "with difficulty" so that we can well imagine him waiting on a suitable opportunity to leave County Antrim and exercising the greatest caution on his journey towards the south.

For the young slave it was a long walk, but the distance was made light, by the knowledge that he was returning home after a separation of years. Fortunately, he travelled without mishap, and in after years, wrote that he "came in the strength of the Lord, who directed his way aright." How he must have prayed on that walk, to a far-off port!

From the shores of Antrim and Down, other boats often sailed across to Scotland, Wales, and England, but Saint Patrick did not want to reach any of these countries. Some of the northern boatmen were known to the slave-boy, but trusting to God to direct his footsteps, he wandered through the country to where he "had never been before" and where he "did not know any of the people." From this statement we naturally conclude, he had been acquainted with other men who "sailed in boats". Arriving, after some days, at the port of departure, the escaping boy was just in time to see the ship make ready for its journey. Approaching the sailors, very nervously, he made known that he wanted to go with them, and "had wherewith to pay" his passage. Some kindly Irish friend had given the young slave the "wherewith" to which he refers, or it may have been sent to him in care of some of the boatmen who sailed from Gaul. On hearing his request, the sailors "looked him over". Probably they realised the lad was a slave to some strong druid, and feared the consequences, if they assisted in his escape. Anyhow the master of the vessel was displeased, and very sharply answered, "you by no means need seek to go with us."

To a boy who had come so far and risked so much, this must have been a great disappointment. He was evidently broken-hearted, for in tears and prayer, he turned from the shore and began to walk back towards a cottage, where the poor inhabitants had been kind to him and had given him food. As he walked, he prayed fervently and before he had proceeded far, was

Irish Wolfhound

overjoyed to hear the voice of some of the people, who were watching the boats make ready, calling after him, "Come quickly, for these men call thee." There was no need to call a second time. The boy heard and turning, ran quickly back towards the water, just as the boat put out. Getting a position at the bow, he watched the waves lap upon the shore, as the men pulled to sea. In a short time, he learned that the seamen were pagans, and on the journey, he was given the task of minding the large Irish hounds which they were taking with them to sell in Gaul. With the handling of hounds, the lad Patrick was familiar. Often a dog had been his sole companion, for months on the hillside. Often the dogs had served him in his servitude. Even though the "men were pagans", with such companions as the hounds, the sea trip of "three days and three nights" was made pleasant. Symmachus, a Roman nobleman, has left us a record of how such Irish hounds astonished Rome in those days.

Having reached the port of Gaul, the boat was dragged on shore, and the party, with the dogs, began a long march that lasted for twenty-eight days and took them through a deserted part of the country where "food failed, and hunger prevailed over them."

Once the mission of these pagan dealers was over, Saint Patrick tells ush he, "was again with his parents," who received him as a son and earnestly entreated, "that he would never again depart from them, after the many calamities he had undergone." After so many years of painful separation, what a happy re-union it must have been, and what wonderful stories that prodigal could tell of his experiences in Ireland – the Ireland he could never forget. Hungry and footsore, he had reached his home, and though his father, the proud decurion, felt bitter towards the nation that had wrecked his home, abused his servants and enslaved his son, the liberated boy held nothing but love for the people whom he had grown to know 'in the land of his captivity'. Often, he dreamed of those slaves he had left behind. Often, he thought of the beauty of their Faith, in comparison with the paganism around them.

His father had no patience with the Christian teaching. He was angry when he heard some of the ideas his son had brought back with him and must have often upbraided him. But Patrick never forgot what he had learned. The pictures of his young fellow Christian slaves kneeling at prayer in the secluded corners of the green hills of Ireland were ever haunting him, and he burned with a desire to return, some day, and set them free. With this ambition in his heart, he daily prayed to God for assistance and direction. Then one night, as he tells us, he "saw a vision" a beautiful vision in which he says, "a man called Victoricius, coming as it were from Ireland," brought several letters, one of which he gave to Patrick. On reading it the Saint saw it headed: 'The Voice of the Irish'. Yes, the voice of his little shepherd friends of the hills and valleys far away, and the voice said, "we entreat thee holy youth, that thou mayst come and henceforth walk amongst us." It was then that he recognised it to be, as he says, "the voice of those who were nigh by the Wood of Fochluth, which is by the western sea." Hearing the appeal, he tells us, he was broken hearted and could read no more.

Patrick was never able to forget Ireland, and try though he may to avoid it, was always disturbed in his dreams, by recollections of the Green Isle.

Again and again, he tells us he was aroused from his sleep by, "The Voice of the Irish", which kept calling him back to the Western Isle.

How could he forget the land of his slavery – how could he forget Ireland, when Ireland had given him the Faith? The little pagan boy, who had been stolen from his home by Irish warriors, was now a Christian man imbued with a Christian ideal. His gratitude to the land where he had been punished was unbounded. Listen to what he says, "I did not believe in the one God from my infancy, but I remained in death and unbelief until I was severely chastised." Ireland had chastised the pagan boy and he returned home with the language of the Gael upon his lips, and the love of God in his heart. No wonder, therefore, that when an old man, he should have manfully proclaimed, "I ought not to hide the gift of God, which he bestowed upon me in the land of my captivity," and should add, "For there I earnestly sought Him, and there I found Him, and he preserved me from all iniquity."

Small wonder then that, "The Voice of the Irish" kept ringing in his ears. With a heart full of gratitude for the country that had enslaved him, the young, liberated slave began to prepare for the great mission that was before him.

Christianity in Gaul - Saint Martin of Tours

The story of the entry of Christianity into Gaul is not too clear, but it would appear that its introduction was mainly brought about by the arrival of immigrants from the Eastern Mediterranean countries, who spread all over the Roman world and were especially numerous in Gaul.

Somewhere about the year 177 a Church had been established at the town of Lyons, where soon after, no less than forty-eight Christians suffered martyrdom for the Faith. From that time Gaul made much religious progress.

As the years passed the number of Churches increased rapidly until, in the year 314, we find that a great Council of Gallic Clergy assembled in the town of Arles, where no less than five Bishops from Britain attended.

From this and other early references appearing in Origen and Tertullian writings, it would seem that Christianity had also spread as far as Britain, about the beginning of the third century.

By the time that the year 315 had dawned, there were Bishop sees at Bordeaux, and at Rouen, and a short time later, one at Poitiers. Some sixty years after these developments, learning and letters began to flourish in the West of the Country, and at such places as Poitiers, Toulouse, Angouleme, Bordeaux and Auch, public schools were maintained.

Much of this religious and educational activity took place near Tours, where Saint Patrick was born in the year 389, but his father being a pagan, the boy did not benefit by it. Almost until the year 405, when Patrick was taken captive by Irish raiders, Christian teaching was progressing in his home country. Then shortly after Alaric had launched his attack on Rome, the barbaric age began to set in, and the collapse continued to spread throughout Europe.

On the Rhine, the Roman defenses crumbled, with the result that Germanic hordes moved into Gaul. Pillaging became the order of the day. Men of learning fled to safety. Lands and other valuables were seized, and about the year 406, when Saint Patrick was in Ireland, as a slave, hordes of Alans, Sueves and Vandals, crossed the Rhine, to be followed soon after by the Burgundians and Visigoths, all of whom contributed to creating the destruction to which Saint Patrick referred, when he said, on returning home he had to travel twenty-eight days through a deserted country.

In this invasion and destruction, the Irish and Scotch took part, making extensive raids on the West Coast, during which they had taken the boy Patrick in 405.

To the student of Irish affairs, a casual reference to these conditions is interesting and necessary, because it was in the years that followed the Roman collapse that Christianity made its permanent abode in Ireland.

From the Leyden Glossary and other records, we learn that during the invasions in question, many of the "upper classes" fled from Gaul and found their way to Ireland and Scotland, and from a reference made to Gallic Emigres, by Saint Patrick himself, it is evident that, when he was later engaged in his missionary work in Ireland, a body of scholars, well educated in the Latin tongue, who regarded him with scorn and even questioned the legitimacy of his mission, had been in the country before he arrived. When the young herdsman, who had escaped from his master had come back to Gaul after his long captivity, he found many changes had taken place, and soon learned of the saintly work of Saint Martin of Tours, in his own native town.

Not far from his home stood the great Monastery of Marmoutier, a monument to that Saint's activity, and the most peaceful harbour in a turbulent age.

In Ireland Patrick may have heard of its founder. Some Christian slave who had been baptised by this soldier-saint, may have told him of his work. The fame of Martin had already spread throughout Europe. A Bishopric had been founded at Tours, and one at Poitiers, both places on the Loire.

Saint Hilary, (the first Latin Hymn writer whose work was sung in Ireland) had been Bishop of Poitiers, from about 353 to 368, and his disciple, Saint Martin, Bishop of Tours, from about 371 to 403.

Saint Martin was dead when Patrick arrived home from slavery, but his churches and monasteries were there.

He had spent an active life in the service of God, and the town of Tours was becoming known as Holy Tours.

About the year 361 Martin had begun the Monastery at Liguge, near to the town, and after becoming Bishop had set up "The Greater Monastery", some two miles distant, having also founded Lerins. For his missionary labours he was celebrated, and Sulpicius Severus has left us a worthy record of him.

When Patrick came into Tours, he found it "ringing with the fame of Holy Martin", and it was not long until he made his way towards "the Greater Monastery", where "Martin had taught men to live the life of Angels amidst a barbarous world".

Already there were some of the monks who could talk of Ireland in the language of Gael, and to these Patrick soon unfolded his ambition.

That Saint Patrick received his training in Gaul is quite evident from his writings. In both his Confession and Epistle, he uses Biblical quotations frequently, and according to competent authorities, these show a mixture of Vulgate forms in their Old Latin. This tendency would naturally be in accordance with the Gallic education of his time. Indeed, it is frequently pointed out that in some phases, his work also recalls that of Irenaeus of Lyons (130 - 202), noted for his expansion of Christianity though the southern regions of Gaul. That Patrick entered the Greater Monastery, there appears little doubt, and from that time until his death, the spirit of Saint Martin seems to have enveloped him. Just shortly before he died, Martin had founded another Monastery on the Island of Lerins, off the coast of Gaul, and many of the Monks of Tours went there. Everything that has been written points to Saint Patrick having been on that Island, for some time, and tradition tells us it was here he received the stick, which became known

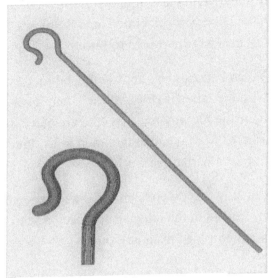

Staff of Jesus

throughout the years by the name of "The Staff of Jesus", because it was believed to have been used by Our Lord himself in Jerusalem. This Monastery of Lerins, in subsequent years, became the most famous of Saint Martin's foundations, and with it, tradition links Saint Patrick strongly. From there, we know that many of the leading ecclesiastics of Gaul were sent out, and to it came disciples from the greater part of the Christian world, including one from Britain, Faustus, who became Abbot from 432 to 450. After being at Tours, Saint Patrick remained here some years to be, for a number of years later, engaged in teaching with Saint Germanus at Auxerre.

Pelagius

In the same year (405) as Saint Patrick had been taken captive to Ireland, a monk – who some have stated was an Irishman, and others have called a Briton – was residing in Rome.

The name given to him by Latin and Greek writers was Pelagius, but his real name was Morgan. Though not a priest, he was a monk of considerable learning, being able to defend himself in the Greek tongue before a Council at Diopolis in 415, while his accuser Orosius, had to employ an interpreter.

Just, as is common in the present age, Morgan was busily engaged in propounding the doctrine of freewill and had many followers.

When six years later, Saint Patrick had escaped from Ireland, Morgan was in Africa with another monk – an Irishman named Kelly, whom Latin and Greek writers called Caelestius. Both were enthusiastically engaged there in a prolonged controversy with a learned deacon called Paulinus, who had accused them of heresy. Pelagius and Caelestius were promoting a system of doctrines which emphasized human choice in salvation and denied original sin. Both of these religious adventurers were born fighters, and commanded attention with their 'heresy' so rapidly that Rome became alarmed.

Saint Jerome dramatically launched his attack upon them, and here is what he said, "An ignorant calumniator has recently broken forth, who thinks that my Commentaries on the Epistle to Saint Paul to the Ephesians, ought to be condemned, and the stupid fellow, heavy with Irish porridge, does not remember what we have said in that very work." Then the controversy raged, and the noted learned men of the period became engaged in it." During the time that Saint Patrick was undergoing his monastic training and, as he says, "humbling himself by hunger", Morgan and Kelly were conducting a vigorous campaign in Europe and were surprising the Christian world by the increasing numbers of their adherents. Their teaching soon inaugurated vast discussion, and Saint Augustine was forced to become its formidable opponent in North Africa.

Into unexpected quarters the doctrine had found its way, and even in Lerins Abbey, an anti-Augustian party arose, with Faustus and John Cassian at its head.

Everyone looked upon this heresy of personal free will as having come from Ireland.

Even Saint Jerome appears to have had that opinion, and Mercator, Prosper and Augustine point particularly to Kelly's Irish birth. Naturally this brought the name of Ireland into great prominence, and into this country came the followers of Morgan and Kelly. Already copies of the Commentary which the has circulated on Saint Paul's Epistles had found their way into Britain, where the Pelagian heresy had taken hold.

In regard to Arianism and Priscillianism having ever reached as far as Ireland, there is little evidence, but with Pelagianism it is an altogether different story. In Irish exegetical manuscripts, its founder is quoted three centuries after his death, and there are various documents of the Pelagian type which point to Irish Pelagian influence. Ranging himself against such religious giants as Saint Augustine and Saint Jerome, Morgan with his love of fighting literally rocked Europe, and he and Kelly found friends. Even with the death of Morgan, the heresy continued.

In the midst of its greatest growth, Saint Germanus was at Auxerre (a resort of Irish Christians for theological study) and with him, fresh from his training at Lerins, was Saint Patrick.

At Arles, Lyons and Rome, Germanus had received the best education of the time, and had been elevated to the position of an Imperial Administrator of Gaul. By Amator, the Bishop of Auxerre, he had been won to religious life, and at Amator's death in 418, he became Bishop of Auxerre, and one of the leading ecclesiastics of his country.

He was a great Missioner, and a man suited in every way to fight the Pelagian heresy, which aroused him to tremendous effort.

In the year 428, after this free-will doctrine had been abroad for over twenty years, and as Germanus viewed the inroads it was making in several countries, a layman of good education, called Prosper of Aquitaine, appeared on the scene. He was a native of Marseilles, where he resided, and was familiar with the trend of events in Gaul. Having been shocked at the growth of

Pelagianism in his own neighbourhood, he wrote a letter to Saint Augustine, describing the situation. In the following year (429) he wrote in his Chronicle: "The Pelagian Agricola, son of the Pelagian Bishop Severianus, corrupts the Churches of Britain by the propagation of his doctrine". Then comes this remark: "But at the instigation of Palladius, Pope Celestine sends Germanus, Bishop of Auxerre, in his stead, who overthrows the heretics, and guides the Britons to the Catholic Faith". Representations may, at this time, have also been made in respect to Ireland.

Germanus had gone to Britain and had rooted out the heresy, bringing back with him the knowledge of how it had been progressing in Ireland.

At the instigation of Palladius, Germanus had been dispatched to Britain, and at the instigation of Germanus, Palladius was later sent to Ireland. From a Life written by Constantius, a priest of Lyons, we learn that Germanus made a profound impression on Britain, and in an appendix to the metrical version of his life, prepared by Heiric of Auxerre, in the ninth century, we discover that he actually had an Irish disciple with him, called Michomere. Michomere, we are sure, made anxious enquiries about his native country, during his successful sojourn in Britain, and must have brought back news to Gaul regarding it – to where Palladius awaited.

Following the success in Britain, it was deemed advisable that the fire of heresy, which was showing some signs of taking a hold in Ireland, should be put out, lest it spread. Someone must be sent. Someone who knew the language. Someone with great courage and great Faith. Saint Patrick was at Auxerre, when Germanus and Michomere arrived back from Britain and were wanting a Missioner for that country, and many historians pretend that he was overlooked; he who knew Ireland, knew it's language, wanted to serve it and forever was hearing, as he tells us, "The Voice of the Irish" calling to him to come.

A suitable emissary had to be found to dispatch to the Irish. Saint Patrick was there and ready to go. Yet we are told by most historians that he was not then sent. This, we shall endeavour to examine in another chapter, for one finds it very difficult to believe that such a man as Saint Patrick proved himself to be could have possibly been overlooked on that occasion and, someone who "didn't know the language", couldn't endure the climate, nor "tolerate a difficulty", should take his place. The two writings which the Saint has left us, convey how desirous he always was to revisit Ireland, and there appears little doubt that he was a particular friend of Germanus. Is it likely, therefore, that he was passed over, and another sent?

At Auxerre, there were some young Irish monks whom Patrick, knowing their language, taught and with Irish traders, he often conversed. Long before that time, there are traces of Irishmen having been at Auxerre, as a certain Corcodemus, in the third century, is particularly mentioned by Constantius, as having come from Ireland.

Even Iserninus, the fellow Bishop of Saint Patrick is also said to have been Irish and was at Auxerre both under Amator and Germanus. When we recall that Saint Patrick, in later years complained of the treachery of a former friend, one wonders if he were a fellow monk who had been an ecclesiastic, to whom, the Saint had at one time communicated his innermost thoughts.

If we try to remember, that when Germanus came back from his successful mission to Britain, he proceeded direct to Auxerre, in Gaul. If we remember that Saint Patrick was at Auxerre when he returned. If we also remember that Saint Patrick knew the language of the Scots (Irish), was continually praying to be sent to them, and he, with his experience of the people; does it not seem strange that another Missioner of the type suggested by most historians, should have been sent in preference to him? In fact, it is not acceptable.

+

ST. PA LL A DI US BISH OP OF IRE LA ND

Palladius

In the previous chapter we read of Prosper having recorded, in the year 429, that "at the instigation of Palladius" Pope Celestine, sent Germanus, Bishop of

Auxerre, to Britain to oppose Pelagianism (the denial of original sin and the rejection of predestination), and direct the Britons to the Catholic faith.

In this we suspect the concern and action of Saint Patrick himself. The realisation of his dream in answer to "the Voice of the Irish" was fast approaching. Already many Irish had settled in Britain. In history, the name Palladius represents a tragic figure. Not having been recognised as Patrick, he is not wanted.

Prosper has described him as a deacon, while the Book of Armagh refers to him as "Chief Deacon to Celestine", possibly because it was, "at his instigation" that the Pontiff sent Germanus to Britain.

This, Palladius, the deacon who so energetically concerned himself about salvation of Britain, we believe to have been none other than the patron Saint of Ireland, Saint Patrick.

Knowing the Irish Apostle from the writings has left us, we can well imagine his anxiety and efforts on behalf of these islands. And we can readily understand the one who wrote the Epistle to Coroticus, making representations to his Holiness on their behalf. At his request, Germanus was dispatched to Britain, where he was appealed to, to send a Bishop to Ireland, and so Saint Patrick was sent. It is then that Prosper, under date 431, makes known that: "Palladius was consecrated by Pope Celestine, and sent as the first

Bishop to the Irish believing in Christ".

Saint Patrick, who had always kept in touch with Ireland, could have told how necessary was such a missioner.

From this record, in Prospers Chronicle, it is clear there were then some "Irish believing in Christ" – the Christian slaves, the stolen Christian women, the converted soldiers and the evicted Gauls. Palladius, then, was Ireland's first Roman Evangelist.

The written story of his experience is somewhat puzzling, but worth examining briefly. From the book of Armagh, we learn, "Palladius, Archdeacon to Pope Celestine, Bishop of Rome, was ordained and sent to convert this island, lying under wintry cold".

In the Vita Secunda, we read, "the most Blessed Pope Celestine ordained to Bishop, the Archdeacon of the Roman Church, named Palladius and sent him to the Island of Hibernia, giving to him, relics of the blessed Peter and Paul, and other Saints, and moreover the volumes of the old and new testaments". Arriving so soon after Germanus's mission to Britain, it would seem certain that Palladius came to Ireland to combat Pelagianism, at the request of the faithful.

And now about this Palladius, who he came to Ireland in the year 431, and who Prosper must have known. Both belonged to Gaul. Palladius was taught in Gaul and Prosper was particularly intimate with affairs in that country. Shortly after Saint Augustine's death, on the 28th of August 430, Prosper had gone to Rome, and was there when this Palladius was sent to Ireland, and probably also met him in the Eternal City. Indeed, from his writings, it looks as if they were personal friends – both having co-operated in pressing for action to be taken against the Pelegian heresy in Britain and elsewhere.

According to the Book of Armagh, Palladius reached Ireland when it was "under winter cold" in 431. Yet it has been asserted, by many historians, that he succeeded in establishing at least three Churches in the South, and disappearing before Saint Patrick is said to have arrived (in the following year). As a matter of fact, he has been made to die quickly by several writers, and

Book of Armagh

hurried into a grave in County Down, so as to provide a sentimental reason for Saint Patrick, to come North to visit his last resting-place.

By some historians we are told he did not stay more than a few days, by others, a few weeks, while some have been more generous and allowed him to remain a few months.

Let us try to examine this more clearly. In the first place, Pope Celestine would have hardly sent a Bishop to Ireland, unless some intimidation had been made to him that such a dignitary was required, and a Bishop so well equipped, as we understand Palladius was, would hardly have come for a few days or months. Furthermore, it is not at all likely that, having come, he would have deserted his flock at the first irritation, as some imply. Remember this is the Palladius who pressed for Germanus to be sent to Britain. It is not easy to accept, therefore, that this outstanding deacon, having been made Bishop of the Irish, came in the winter of 431, and went away after a few months. To him, historians who did not see him as Saint Patrick, have been brutally uncharitable. To have him removed in order to suit a date, they have pictured this courageous Apostle (for it took a courageous Apostle of the Christian Faith to come to Ireland in those days, as you shall learn), running away from his mission and leaving his Bishopric, friends and relics behind him.

Tradition being so strong on his companions having remained behind in Wicklow, it has apparently been too difficult to submerge it, so they were permitted to remain.

About all this there is a decided ring of un-reliance. All kinds of excuses have been offered. All kinds of strange conclusions arrived at. Surely there must be some explanation for the hundred and one attempts made to get Palladius out of the way at all costs. To make the Life of Patrick easy, may have been an intention with some, but they have in reality, only succeeded in making his life more difficult.

From the book of Armagh, we learn that the natives upset him. Here is what it says: "But he was unsuccessful, for one can receive anything from earth, unless it be given him from heaven, and neither did these fierce barbarians receive his doctrine readily, nor did he himself wish to remain long in a land not his own".

Of his work, for the short time he is said to have been in Ireland we learn from the Scholiast on St. Fiacc's Hymn that "he founded some Churches, viz: Teach-na-Roman, or, House of the Romans, Killfine and others". The same authority also informs us: "he was not well received by the people but was forced to sail".

In ancient times, the headland of Howth appears to have been a well-known landing place for foreigners coming to Ireland. Near there, Palladius and his companions had arrived, as the Vita Secunda tells us: "at the territory of the men of Leinster, where Nathi Mac Garrehon was chief, who was opposed to him". The Vita goes on: "Others however, whom the Divine Mercy" had disposed towards the worship of God, having been baptised in the name of the Sacred Trinity. The blessed Palladius built three churches in the same district, one which is called Killfine (i.e. the Church of Finte, perhaps the present Dunlavin) in which, even to the present day, he left his books received from Saint Celestine, and the box of relics of S.S. Peter and Paul and other saints, and tables on which he used to write, which in Irish are called for his name, Pallere – that is, the burden of Palladius, and are held in veneration. Another was called Teach-na-Roman, the House of the Romans, and the third, Dumnach-Ardech (Donard near Dunlavin) in which repose the holy companions of Palladius, viz., Sylvester and Salonius who are still honoured there".

In spite of all this, we are asked to believe that the Chief Nathi Mac Garrehon, chased Palladius from Wicklow and allowed his companions to remain. It is really too absurd to credit.

As if ignoring the admitted establishing of at least three Churches, and the continuance of the mission by Sylvester and Salonius and others, the Vita Quarta, makes this strange reference: "The Almighty had not predestined the Irish people to be brought by him from the errors of heathenism to the Faith".

Because of the inability to accept Palladius as Patrick, no end of confusion has arisen and existed through the years. Writers have been at their wits end to get Palladius out of the way quick, with painful result and increasing confusion. The book of Armagh dramatically describes his exit, thus: "wherefore he returned to him who sent him. On his way, however, having begun his land journey, he died in the territory of the Britons". Presumably on his way back to Rome or Gaul. Palladius was not wanted by the scribe.

The Scholiast does not get him out of the way so quickly, as it says: "after leaving Wicklow, he sailed around the coast towards the North, until he was driven by a tempest to the land of the Picts (Scotland) where he founded the Church of Fordun, and there he is known by the named of Pledi". The Vita Secunda also reports his arrival there and says: "after a short time Palladius died at Fordun, but others say he was crowned with martyrdom there". The Vita Quarta puts it more delicately, by simply saying: "he migrated to the Lord in the region of the Picts". Muirchu, one of the first to mention him, just says he died and several others "he died of disease". That "he was forced to go round the coast towards the North" is how one life describes his departure, as if Palladius would have sailed to Scotland, if he were resigning his Bishopric, and returning to

Rome or Gaul. Irish writers did not want Palladius.

Unfortunately for these historians, Fordun in Scotland had an unassailable traditional link with Palladius. He

CÆLESTINVS·IIII·PP·MEDIOLA·

Pope Celestine

had been there, and so by any device, he must be got there before he passed out, even though he were fleeing from Ireland. Indeed, it is surprising to what extremes some of the opinions of Palladius have gone. We learn of him that he "had no tact". Mark you! The man who pleaded with Pope Celestine. We are told he did not know Irish. As if, even in that year, a Bishop knowing the language could not have been found. It is said "he failed". As if he did not know to where he was coming, what was expected from him, and the difficulties he had to surmount. The "Irish believing in Christ" also awaited him.

Some tell us he "deserted his post", others that he "ran away from his Bishopric" and left his companions in danger, as if the great deacon Palladius, so highly honoured by his Holiness, Pope Celestine, were such a man.

Now, when we recall that Prosper, who recorded the coming of Palladius to Ireland in 431, was in Rome, and did not make this entry until 433, it seems strange that, if Palladius were a failure, or was dead, that he did not refer to this. But that is not all. At a later date 437, six years after this journey of Palladius, Prosper wrote again, and in his statement, there is no reference whatever to failure or death; on the contrary, he pays tribute to the success of the Palladius mission in Ireland. Do not forget, therefore, that at that time Saint Patrick had been, as admitted by nearly all historians, five years in the country. Where then, we might ask was Palladius and where was Patrick? Prosper knew nothing of Palladius, and where was Patrick? Prosper knew nothing of Patrick but apparently watched with interest, the progress of Palladius. To the Irish, Palladius may or may not have been known as Patricius, but to Prosper, his name was Palladius.

No satisfactory explanation can be offered for the two names, but Palladius could have been the family name by which he had been known to Prosper, while Patricius might have been his title or baptismal name. although, as you have learned, Prosper concerned himself, very earnestly, about the progress of Christianity in Gaul, Britain and Ireland, and made special note of Palladius in 431, it is very singular that he never once mentioned the bishop Patrick, who is said to have come from his country Gaul in the year 432. Again, if Palladius, the first Bishop of Ireland, had been martyred for the Faith, would it have been unreasonable to expect that Saint Patrick, who is said to have followed him so closely, would have mentioned him in some of his writings, and awakened a devotion to him like that which was enkindled to Saint Martin of Tours? More particularly as so many insist, he specially went North to be near his grave.

In connection with Palladius, it is very singular, that when his name was forgotten by the Irish, it should be remembered by the Scotch. On no Irish Calendar of Saints, does his name appear, yet in the Breviary of Aberdeen, it is entered under July 6th.

Even to this day the church founded by Palladius in Scotland, is known not by his name, but by Paddie's Church" while the fair held in commemoration of his work and residence among the Picts of the Highlands, is known as "Paddie's fair". The Scotch remembered him when the Irish had forgotten, and tradition in connection with the "Fair" and "Church" points clearly to his having also been once recognised as Patrick by very early generations.

Patrick, I have tried to prove, came from Gaul, and it is generally accepted that Palladius also came from there. It is curious therefore to discover under the date 16th March, the day before Saint Patrick's Day, in the Roman Martyrology, the name of Patrick, Bishop, who was commemorated at Averni or Clermont, in Gaul, the very country where Palladius was said to have come from, by those who have made Patrick Scotch, English or Welsh. The words of the entry are: "Avernis S. Patriccu episcopi" and it is not said he was Bishop of Auvergne, but only that his deposition, that is, his death, was on that day commemorated, Cardinal Baronius tried to unearth a Patrick amongst the Bishops

Wicklow Mountains

of Clermont but was unable to do so.

I have already pointed out, that Palladius and Patrick came from the same country. Both, it is asserted, were with Germanus at Auxerre. Both sailed from Gaul. Both brought several companions. Both lived at the same time. Both arrived at Wicklow.

One, it is said, reached Ireland in the winter of 431, the other sometime in 432. Palladius stayed a short while in the South. Patrick stayed there a short while also. The principal reason offered for Palladius's speedy departure is that he was chased. There is no reason offered for Patrick's. The same chieftain was in Wicklow, (Nathi Mac Garrehon) when both arrived, and he could have hardly become so friendly to Christian Missioners, within a few months. When Palladius sailed north, Patrick also sailed in the same direction. Palladius went to the Scots in Scotland, but Patrick landed with the Scots in Ulster. Does not this short comparison admit confusion?

Pelagius, as I have said, was known to the Britons as Morgan. Celestius, to the Scots, as Kelly. And why not Palladius to the Irish as Patrick? How many of our Irish Saints are known to us by the true form of their names? From the very earliest times, the persistent use of familiar pet names, or nicknames, seems to have been a characteristic of Irish society. Why not, then, Palladius the Patrician? Indeed, everything points to this confusion having arisen as a result of the desire to divide Patrick, so that both Scotland and Ireland should be served by two separate Saints of their own.

Palladius, by Scotch historians, was made to arrive in Scotland, and never leave it again. Patrick was placed in Ireland, by Irish writers, and there he remained until he died.

In this attitude, national prejudice no doubt had something to say. Fortunately, there are several able historians, much removed from this influence, who have seen Patrick in Palladius. Loofs, Schoell, Zimmer and others maintain they were the same person, the latter writer regarding the name Palladius as a Roman rendering the name of Sucatus, by which Patrick had been also known.

Saint Patrick, it must be mentioned, always prided himself on his Roman rank, and we have an old Irish authority that tells us, his name Patrick was not a real name, but the name of a rank amongst the Romans.

In the writings of the elder Cuimine, a disciple of Saint Columba, who wrote about the end of the sixth century, we make an interesting discovery. This learned man reveals that Patrick was the first Apostle of Ireland. What then of Palladius? Apart altogether from such references, and no doubt written from most reliable information, we have a paragraph, added by Ferdomnach, to the copy of Tirechan, which definitely states that "Palladius, the Bishop, is first sent, who by another name was called Patrick".

Evidently the people of Ferdomnach's day believed this, and up to the time of the writing of the first Lives of Saint Patrick, had no confusion, whatever in their minds. When, however, after over two hundred years, the historians took up the task of writing, they found it difficult to fit in the record of Prosper's Palladius, in the year 431, with the Patrick of the two Latin documents, the Confession and Epistle, which had been preserved, or did not want to. Yet, for many years it would appear, from both Ferdomnach and the elder Cuimine, the Irish people had regarded Palladius as Patrick.

Later writers, most of whom, would not allow themselves to believe that the Irish Warriors of 405 could carry a thousand captives from Gaul to Ireland, continued the struggle of trying to prove that Patrick's place of capture and birth was Scotland. Others not being able to surmount the Gallic tradition, admitted he was born in Gaul, but had been "on holidays" in Scotland, when he was taken. Of course, some reason had to be found for him being there, and kind authors suggested he was with relations. On subsequent histories of the Saint, these and various other conclusions had injurious effects.

Having once decided that Patrick was born in Scotland, and as the Saint in his Confession conveyed that he never returned home, it was then concluded he never visited that country, whereas, "Palladius" did really go there, and Portpatrick and other places, as well as tradition, are evidence of Patrick's visits.

Again, in respect to Palladius, Scotch history insists that he was a Bishop of the Scots of Scotland, for at least twenty-four years, and tradition there reminds us, that Termanus was baptised by him, in his infancy, and afterwards consecrated Archbishop by him.

If, therefore, he baptised Termanus, when he was a child and later on consecrated him an Archbishop, Palladius could not have disappeared so mysteriously as Irish writers assert; on the contrary, he must have lived to a fairly ripe old age and been a most successful and persevering Missioner.

That he was Patrick, and that Patrick, who was first Bishop of the Scots, (in those days the Irish) went to and from Scotland, which was then a colony of the Irish, and was really regarded as part of Ireland, is the convinced opinion of the writer.

Such an Apostle was Patrick, the first Bishop of all the Scots of Ireland, Scotland, Isle of Man, Wales, and England.

The Ireland Saint Patrick Came To

"An Irish Empire"

The Isle of Saints and Scholars

When Saint Patrick came as Bishop, to Ireland in the
year 431, he came fully equipped; ready, not merely to

purchase his own freedom from his former master, Miliucc, but to pay for the freedom of other Christian slaves.

In his Epistle, he himself tells us: "It is the custom of the Roman and Gallic Christians to send holy and suitable men to the Franks and other nations, with so many thousands of solidi (worth about eight shillings) to redeem baptised slaves". If we read this aright, we have one of the reasons for the coming of Saint Patrick. Ireland had many, very many Christian slaves. Ireland had many noble families and noble children were above work. As he tells us, he could never forget the voices of those with whom he had been once enslaved, "by the Western Sea" and, as if in answer to their prayers and call, he came to set them free.

How proud, therefore, and yet how thankful to God he must have been, when he and his companions set sail from Gaul upon their glorious mission? The slave-boy of former years was coming back a bishop and returning to liberate his friends and convert the pagans.

One wonders if a whisper of his coming had drifted to the hard boys on the Irish hills, and if as they looked out towards the sea, they knelt in prayer for his protection on the journey.

What congregation awaited the new Bishop? Herding sheep and tending dogs, were scattered Christians, as well as some of the pagan Chiefs wives, or Christian mothers. There were seamen who knew of God. The Gallic troubles had driven others into the country, and there were a few followers of Pelagius, whose teachers had been in Ireland. These were all principally resident along to eastern coast. The remainder of the people were pagan. The Kings and Chiefs were pagan.

Divided as the Irish were into tribes or clans, that occupied various districts, they were happy, haughty and fairly comfortable people.

About 1,000,000 populated the island, and all of the men and youths were warriors, trained to battle and trained to endure.

With each tribe, pride of race was pre-eminent, every member boasting of a common glorious ancestor. Even to-day, this pride of clan remains in Ireland, where there is still "no stalk like the old-stalk".

Tara was the seat of government and there the High King of Ireland reigned.

At the coming of Saint Patrick as Bishop, Laoghaire, a son of Niall of the Nine Hostages, occupied the Throne. He was a pagan, as also were his cousins and sons who were minor Kings in other parts of the country at the same time.

Of the chieftains, there does not appear to have been any Christians, and all the Kings we know of, were undoubtedly pagan, when the Saint arrived to preach the Gospel.

As a result of this condition, the Druids were very powerful. Pagan worship was prevalent, and the stone circles, the high mounds, the pillar-stones etc., which we still can see around us in Ireland today, are reminders of the worship that Saint Patrick met on his arrival. In it the sun, moon and stars formed and important part. Of the beliefs, the Saint himself speaks when he says: "That sun whom we behold rises daily at the command of God for our use." The Druids, he explained, could not, as some believed, influence the Sun. Even the name of Grian, in some of our Irish towns, reminds us of the existence of that worship. In Granard, County Meath, there was a famous Druid's well at the time Saint Patrick came, and for many years before then, a huge sun altar had existed and Greenore Point in County Wexford.

Everywhere throughout the land, there were pagan gods, pagan wells, pagan costumes, pagan ornaments, pagan countries, Ireland had no human sacrifice, which very probably, proved the reason why those who followed the Saint, were so successful and why Ireland, after his death, became so religious.

The Druids being the learned men of the time, had control of the learned professions, so were judges, teachers, physicians, prophets, and poets.

Sometimes, during Saint Patricks wanderings in the country, he was obliged to pay heavy fines which they imposed upon him, for to them, this Christian Bishop was a rebel and often broke the laws. He was also a suitable victim to plunder.

Actually, the Druids were the nation's only teachers, and as the Kings, Princes and Chieftains had confidence in them, they entrusted their sons and daughters to them for instructions.

Saint Patrick came to supplant these men and to supply Christian Teachers, thus accounting for the violent opposition he met with.

On all occasions, these Druids acted as advisers to the Kings and the people. In previous years they may have "invoked the powers" to ensure the safety and success of the great roving mission that had brought back the boy Patrick captive. Now they were confronted with the slave of Slemish as Champion of Christianity.

They were the teachers of religion. For centuries they had been regarded as mighty magicians, who could do wonderful things, as all our stories of them tell us.

So dominant had they become, and so convinced were the trusting warrior-people of their power, that it was believed they could control the air, sea and weather, could make fog, bring showers of rain or snow, awaken thunder and lightning, cause storms etc.

Like the Greek and Roman Augurs and Soothsayers, the Irish Druids foretold the future, read the stars, interpreted dreams, put words to the songs of the birds, found meaning in the piping of the frog, the croaking of the raven etc., and could drive men insane with a "madman's wisp". "By the Sun", these learned pagans swore, and this became a practice with the people. We have the story of King Laoghaire swearing by the sun that he would never raid Leinster again, and on breaking his oath, being killed by sunstroke. There is also the record of Cormac Mac Art, who, having laughed at the Druids, was choked by the bone of a fish.

Undoubtedly, they were powerful people, whose influence even today, is felt in some of the Irish and Scotch superstitions.

The sun, fire, and water were made of great use by them. The sun they, like Joshua, could influence. Fire they could direct, and the wells were sacred, having power over sickness and death. But most terrible of all, they had "cursing stones", and these possessed a terrorising influence on people.

Often, we are sure, they cursed Saint Patrick and the early Christians without avail.

To the pagan Irish, Tara was their stronghold, and around it everything centred. To it, bards came with their songs; Chieftains with their stories; traders with their bargains; visitors with their gifts and warriors with their prisoners. It was a magnet to all Ireland. Tara shone when Saint Patrick arrived, and he laboured with success to make Armagh outshine Tara.

At the root of the nature worship, Saint Patrick struck, simply by telling, that God was greater than the sun and that he controlled the sun, moon, and the stars. As he preached, the people awaited the curses of the Druids to fall, and seeing him survive, they wondered. When the snow fell at Tara, the Druids claimed they caused it, whereupon Saint Patrick modestly asked them to have it removed. For the first time someone dared to seriously question their power.

There is every reason to believe that when the Saint arrived in Ireland, to challenge these Druids, he found the higher-class had learned the art of writing and must have discovered many skilled in the art of working with metals.

Before his coming, Pagan Brehons appear to have actually had law books, and we know that the saint himself, kept as part of his household, goldsmiths, braisers and other artists, to make crosses, croziers, chalices, bells and such like.

In securing the services of skilled workmen, therefore, he experienced little difficulty. Once, having converted the pagan craftsmen, he was able to command the service of their hands in helping forward Christian work.

On account of the worship of the sun, moon and stars, the pagan Irish, who were fond of wearing ornaments, had articles of gold in crescent shape and circular form, the former class of broach or pendant being worn during the moon's first quarter.

The natives loved colours and this fondness manifested itself in their dress. The higher the grade of society, the louder the colour. Glasheens and other plants were cultivated with which to die the cloths. Furs of animals, like seals, badgers, foxes etc., were extensively used. All the wearing material worn by both sexes was made at home by able hands. Saint Patrick found these workers of great service in replenishing his monastic wardrobes as the number of his Churches grew.

The country was traversed by five great roads over which he travelled in his chariot, and on which at suitable positions, were Brewys, or Hostels for the traveller. On either hand, large herds of cattle could be seen in the charge of shepherd slaves. Beautiful woods bedecked the hillsides on which the chieftains had their ringed-in strongholds. In picturesque spots, the small wattles-made dotted the land.

Skilled in the art of fishing, the twining rivers were the haunt of many fishermen, while those who worked the land, seemed ever to be busy in the fields.

It was a well-doing, well organised community that Saint Patrick had come to save. The age was a fighting one, and the powerful Irish Chieftains, who had braved the conquering Roman legions in Scotland, to where they had rushed to help their Scottish friends, had made a name for themselves. During all the years, that the Romans had tramped in Britain, they had been daily expecting invasion, and were prepared to give resistance. Scotland was also theirs in those days. A famine in the third century had driven many of their people to that country. When the Romans threatened Scotland, therefore, the Irish had rushed across to save their kinsmen. So annoying had they been to the Romans, that a great wall was built at the Firth of Clyde, and another at Solway Firth, to provide protection against their repeated attacks.

Undoubtedly, they must have been formidable. Eumenius, in speaking of Caesar, might remark: "After so many glorious exploits, he (Caesar) disdained to seize Ireland", but this explanation reads as if even Eumenius himself, realised how tremendous would have been the resistance of these Irish to such an invasion.

It is more likely that, even the mighty Caesar, measured the cost of such an undertaking. Anyhow, the military power of Rome never conquered Ireland, but the gentle power of Patrick did.

In the year of the Saint's coming, Ireland was no mean nation. There was no British Empire then to drown it, and the Roman Empire had failed to do so.

It was a free, independent, and vigorous country – and even something more than that.

A little over fifty years before the Saint appeared as a Bishop, its great King Criffan had been recognised, not merely as King of Ireland, but as "King of Ireland and Albion to the British Channel." In ancient records, this is how he is described, and we know that high chieftains of Scotland came to pay him homage.

Of attacks made on Britain in 360, Marcellinus, gives us some information, so that, even the presence of the mighty legions of the Roman Empire in that country then, did not daunt the Irish warriors.

After King Criffan, came Niall of the Nine Hostages, who reigned from 379 to 405. For Foreign conquests he also was distinguished, invading Britain in more extensive scale than his predecessor. Over a large extent of that country, he and his army swept, carrying back immense stocks of booty and whole crowds of captives, to work in the Irish fields and attend the Irish cattle.

At the beginning of the fifth century the martial powers of Rome began to wane. Between the years 402 and 407, the Roman troops were withdrawn from Britain to the Continent. Then the Irish cheered and prepared to build "an Empire".

Had the great Saint Patrick not appeared in the very midst of their preparations and had not the people so speedily embraced the Faith, who can say, but that the world might have had an Irish Empire. Instead, we had an Empire of Christianity. The isle of the Saints and Scholars, for, "from the fifth to the eleventh century, Ireland became the teacher of Europe, and instead of warriors, sent forth illustrious sages, whose names illuminate the dark night of ignorance and barbarism". The warrior was replaced by the priest, and the priest traversed where the warrior had battled.

In the present day, we do not realise how near the world was to having such a power, but there still are documents and undeniable traces of its forming. As I have said, with the withdrawal of the Roman from Britain, the Irish cheered. Already, Scotland was Ireland's country. Across the narrow sea the warriors streamed continuously. Then into Britain, the Irish assisted by the Scotch ventured, where in North Wales, South Wales, and the Cornish Peninsula they soon established themselves. Holyhead, of which the Welsh name means, "the Rocks of the Galls" became an Irish stronghold. Circular forts like those in their native country were erected, and these rings, even until today, arc called the "Irishmen's Cottages". Moreover, the Welsh language contains a number of words that were borrowed from the Irish, who once ruled there.

Into various parts of Britain, the extending nation sent

its armies. In their advance, the Isle of Man was taken and there at present, is seen to be one of the few round towers, to be found outside Ireland, to tell of an Irish colony.

With the advance of the fighting race into other countries there was panic, and many Britons fled to Gaul.

Over Europe, the raids and conquests of the Irish were spoken of. They were an unconquered and conquering people. They were known to be fierce and fearless, one Latin writer actually saying that Irish mothers gave the first food to their baby boys on a sword point as a kind of dedication to war.

For years they swept all before them, and wandered where they liked, some raiding Gaul and others venturing as far as to the Alps. Ancient authors of Carthage, Greece and Rome tell us of these extensive movements.

Gildas, a British historian, relates: "that whole armies of Irish were often seen landing on the British shores in curraghs" and an ancient Irish writer says that: "during a certain military expedition the sea between Ireland and Scotland looked as if covered with a continuous bridge of curraghs".

This was the kind of expedition that visited Gaul and took Saint Patrick back as captive, so no one might be surprised at the number of slaves it secured.

The activity of these vigorous Irish soldiers must have been tremendous, and the territory over which they held sway much larger than is credited.

Remember that Porphyry, at the end of the third century, had described the Irish tribes as being the inhabitants of the whole Britannic world. In far off Rome, they were regarded even at that time, as a powerful nation.

How much greater, then, must they have been with the collapse of the Roman Empire? Britain was then "on the run" before the armies of Ireland. Much of their choicest lands were taken. Thousands of their people rushed to Gaul. To the weakening Lords of Rome, who had protected them so long, they called for assistance. The Irish were taking hold of their country.

It was then that the Roman General, Stilicho, came to help them. Of him a Roman poet, speaking as Britannia, says: "By him was I protected, when the Irish (Niall) moved all Ireland against me and the ocean foamed with hostile oars."

The Irish were feared. They held many places. Ireland was almost an "Imperial Power." Then Patrick came, and in a few years the warlike efforts ceased, for Gildas tells us, there were no more raids after the year 446. No country was so much effected and so quickly changed by Christian teaching. Plundering gave way to praying. Fighting gave way to Faith. Hatred was supplanted by love. The warriors laid down their swords and raised their crosses. Ireland was transformed by a miracle.

Over the ground that had been trampled by the dreaded Pagan Irish warriors, came the silent bare footsteps of the Christian Monks. To where the soldiers had prepared the way to Missioner followed. Into Scotland, the Isle of Man, Wales, England, Spain, France and as far as the Alps, the Irish soldiers of Christ proceeded to win for their country the honoured name of *The Isle of Saints and Scholars.*

Hostility towards Saint Patrick

When Saint Patrick, piloted by Irish seamen, came as Bishop to Ireland in the winter of 431, he had with him twelve companions.

The expedition was well equipped for its mission and was not so hurriedly dispatched as it has been made to appear.

When the Saint and his friends left the shores of Gaul on their eventful journey, they encountered rough weather, as we know that, at least, one of the boats that constituted "the fleet" was long delayed.

Taking the already well-known route from Gaul towards the Howth Headland, the new Bishop and his party arrived at Inbher De (now Wicklow Harbour) where the historians say "Palladius" had also landed.

How long Saint Patrick remained in this district we do not know, but there appears little doubt that he did not, as is said, "just touch land" and then "go North".

The Saint had been in Ireland before. Knew something of the country. For years he had kept in touch with it, and undoubtedly had Irish Missioners with him.

When he reached Wicklow, therefore, he was received by some residents who gave him welcome. These may have been mainly Christian slaves or pagan's Christian wives, but it would be too absurd to assert, as too many writers have done, that the Saint "just called" "did not delay" and "immediately went North".

To read the Saint's own writings, is to understand what manner of man he was, and he was not one to either, "just call and pass on" or to be terrorised by the Chief Nathi, who was made the bogeyman for "Palladius's removal".

Saint Patrick did more than "just call" at Wicklow. He landed with his companions and spent the remainder of the winter in that district, where he established several churches, of which three are credited in history to "Palladius". For some months he was busy in that locality.

At the first sign of summer, the Saint and some of his companions then sailed North, to where they were piloted by the skillful boatmen of the coast. For the Bishop of Scots, the North was the most suitable part of the country.

Efforts, that appear to have been foolish, are made to describe the Saint coming to Ireland in a tremendous hurry. He has been pictured as if waiting on the news of the death of Palladius, to receive the call. The moment he hears of it, he rushes off. Yet, as I have previously said, "Palladius" did not die for many years later.

Saint Patrick did not come to Ireland in a hurry. Some time was required to prepare for such an ambitious undertaking as the conversion of the Irish Race. Ecclesiastical gear, for the equipment of the new communities, had to be provided. Vestments and other cargoes of spiritual treasures had to be made ready. Large sums of money to be gathered.

We do know of the provisions made by Pope Gregory for the mission of Saint Augustine to England, and we learn from Saint Patrick's own writings that he must have had much solidi (eight shillings) with him, when he came.

The mission had to be financed and the Christians of Rome and Gaul did the financing, as they were accustomed to doing in those days. Leaving some of his companions to continue the good work he had commenced in the South, the Saint sailed North, and we prefer to believe that his reason for doing so, so soon after his arrival, was not because of any action of Chief Nathi Mac Garrehon, but because he believed that part of Ireland was the most serviceable and suitable, for the conducting of his mission, being more convenient to Scotland. No doubt he also wished to have himself made right with the Law in respect to slaves. Remember he had been a slave, and had escaped, so naturally would have desired to see his old master Miliucc in order to procure his freedom, possibly by purchasing it.

To a very small colony of humble fishermen that lived along the banks of Strangford Lough, in County Down, is mainly due the fact of Saint Patrick's arrival at that particular place, in the year 432. For Christian Missioners the Irish Kings and Chieftains had no time, but the humble men of Strangford who sailed the seas – and heard on their journeys, whispers of a Christ, who had walked the shores of Galilee with other humble fishermen and died upon a Cross – had come back with the pearls of thought they gathered from the ocean, to unfold them, in secret, by the long lough-shore.

Strangford Lough

In those days the seamen of Strangford were the most skilled of all the Irish, and visited foreign countries often, being also frequent visitors to Scotland.

The strong varying currents of their native waters had trained them to battle the sea, and they wandered far.

Along the lough-shore they had their quaint artistic little wattle-homes, and to them, from their wanderings, they brought many things. Stories of the outside world. Coins of foreign power. Tales of a crucified Christ. Money to free a slave. This time, however, they brought Saint Patrick and his companions when they had rowed from Wicklow.

Too much has been made, by historians, of the Saint's association with Kings and Chieftains, but we must not forget that the Irish Kings were pagans when Saint Patrick arrived in Ireland, and remained so until long after his death, while very few of the Chieftains were his worst enemies. They denounced him. They were not his friends. Saint Patrick was essentially the Saint of the Irish poor. He found his friends amongst the lower orders.

Like his divine master, he began his great mission with the humble men of the sea and made the shores of Strangford the Irish Galilee. How happy he must have been amongst them is proved by his consistent love for that district. He lived there and not at Tara or Armagh.

When the little boats, bearing himself and his friends came sailing across the Strangford Lough towards the little river Slany, we can imagine the anxious faces on the shore.

From Saint Patrick's Confession, we know that crowds of people used to congregate in order to watch these seamen come and go.

How strange a sight it must have been, therefore, to those who stood at the water's edge on that occasion, to behold the boats bearing Ireland's first Bishop and his priest's approach, the strange garbs of the Missioners, showing in great contrast to the rough skins of the sturdy boatmen.

Often in earlier years these strong arms had pulled-in plunder from another land. This time they carried back a Saint and made him welcome. Who knows but that Saint Patrick may have met that day, a boy, then grown to manhood, with whom he had played in his days of minding cattle?

News of the arrival of the white-robed strangers with their shaven-heads soon spread. What would the chieftains do? Would they resent the presence of these newcomers? Would they defy the Druids and make the Christians welcome? Would they chase them from the shores?

To the rough seamen of Strangford, such questions presented themselves, but the new Bishop feared not. Humble as he was, he felt at home with humble people and happy to find in County Down, a welcome from the poor. With them he made his home and in their modest houses found hospitality. In their little boats he and his companions went out fishing, and in the quietness of the evenings, along that blessed shore, he told his first small, but earnest audience of seafarers, the message of his Divine Master.

For days he was harboured in their homes, but the good simple folk soon erected a place of habitation for their first Bishop. Small it must have been, but we are sure it was made comfortable by those early Irish Christians, who at every moment, dreaded the coming of pagan chiefs, and anxiously watched over the gentle strangers, lest they should be attacked.

No doubt a boat, oft-times, lay ready on the lough to bear them off to safety, in case the fierce chieftains came to destroy them.

Not far from the historic spot where the Saint had landed and lived, there resided a strong chieftain. His name was Dichu, and he was a pagan. Overall that district, including the shores of the lough, he reigned. Very soon he heard of the presence of the white-robed strangers in his domain, and he was angry, but being a man who had sailed the seas and talked with men of other lands, he had learned something of the growth of Christianity.

To Christians, however, he did not take easily for he feared the power of the Druids. Hearing of the arrival of the Missioners, he commanded them to appear before him, in explanation of their presence. To him Saint Patrick went. Walking along the paths, accompanied by two friends, the Saint, on approaching Dichu's home, was met by a number of large hounds, they barked angrily. Saint Patrick, in the days of his slavery, had handled such dogs, and showing no fear, was soon seen patting them on the heads. This surprised the Chieftain, who, speaking to the Saint, was further astonished to discover that he addressed him in his native tongue. Dichu had heard of these Christian Missionaries before. He was a wise man of his time. He also was aware that many of the men of the Lough shore, knew of the Christian Faith and that some of them possessed it. But still he dreaded the Druids, and stories he had heard made him also fear the Christian Missioners. He was kind, however, and when the Saint asked him for permission to remain and erect a Church by the shore, he gave him that permission, and with it a wooden erection not far from his own home.

The people knew it as a barn, and so the site is known by the name of Saul today.

Here Saint Patrick founded a Church, and from here his great work began in earnest.

He and his companions had undertaken to convert a pagan people and that they met with much hostility, that the new religion was fiercely resented and that he and his priests suffered much abuse, we know from the Saint's own writings.

Many of the Historians of Saint Patrick attempt to convey that the Saint spent most of his time in the company of Kings and Chieftains. Efforts are made to convince us that he even co-operated with Kings in making laws. All this is far from the truth. The Saint was a simple man who came with the simple faith, to teach a simple people.

In the humble homes he found his hearers and with the humble folk he built his Church, in spite of the Kings, Chieftains and learned Druids, who formed his greatest opposition.

For proof of this, we only require to read the Saint's own writings and to remember that the many attempts upon his life came not from the humble Irish, but from the ruling classes.

"I did not go to Ireland until I was worn out," Saint Patrick tells us, and the work of converting a people of unusually strong convictions was no easy task for an old man.

Many times, I am sure, he was glad to get back from his labours to the restful solitude of Saul. In time his neighbour, the Chieftain, Dichu, became more friendly with his Missioners. From them he learned of many things in far-off countries. From them he learned of the sacrifice our Saviour made upon the Cross. Often, he had deigned to talk to the gentle, white-robed strangers. Then one day, the district around Saul was thrilled by the news that the great pagan Chieftain Dichu, had been baptised by Saint Patrick.

Dichu was the first Irish Chieftain to be received into the Faith by the Saint himself, and while he lived, he always gave ready assistance and protection to the "zealous holy men", who were his neighbours. He was one of the few Chieftains who befriended to the new Bishop and Priests.

At times, when they required it, his strong arm was their protection, and his children and warriors sometimes escorted the Saint to other parts of the country in order to provide a guard for him. When he died Saint Patrick lost a friend.

"Bound," as he tells us, "Not to see again any of my kindred," Saint Patrick made Saul his home and headquarters. There he baptised his first and perhaps his last Chieftain. There he spent the greater part of his life, and there, we are told, he died.

From it, each day, he and his companions went forth amongst the people, speaking to the slave-boy on the hills, enquiring, regarding the slave-men of the fields, or visiting the humble scattered homes of the common people. Saint Patrick loved Saul and from it organised his long battle for the Faith, a battle of love and kindness against hatred, abuse and cruelty. It was undoubtedly a struggle that entailed much sacrifice and many trials.

For some reason there is a notion abroad that the Irish people rallied to him at once, that he was feted by the

Kings and Princes and that he died leaving almost the entire population Christian. Nothing could be further from the truth. Saint Patrick endured much and was tortured so continuously by violent opposition that a less saintly and less courageous man would have been forced to resign his Bishopric, as has been suggested in respect to Palladius.

But the consolation and gratitude that he received from the poor slaves and poor fishermen always gave him hope in his darkest hours, and from them he received encouragement.

The Kings and learned Druids might scoff at his teaching, but the poor and untutored welcomed it.

To his humble barn at Saul, those who had already received the Faith, came in the silence of the night to pray and listen to the inspired message of the Missioners, while others came to be converted.

Soon, throughout the entire area, now known as County Down, the "white strangers" became talked of, and people came to see and hear them.

As a little foreign boy on the hills of County Antrim, Saint Patrick had often seen and examined the curious little shamrock plant. As a youth he must have been particularly observant. How, in illustrating the mystery of the Trinity to the simple minds of his hearers, his early observation stood him in good stead. Holding the little green three-leaf plant aloft in his fingers, he used it to illustrate his references to the Holy Trinity for those who gathered in County Down to hear him. This, he repeated wherever he went, until, at last the shamrock took on a new and nobler meaning to the people of the island.

Around the shores of Strangford his voice resounded as continually proclaiming his unworthiness, he modestly preached: "he who is mighty came and in his own mercy raised me and lifted me up". What a contrast to the boasting of the Kings, the Druids and the Princes! No wonder the poorer people came to his. Time padded by, but already the Saint had paid a visit to County Antrim, where he learned that his old master Miliucc, had died, having been burned in his home. His children, those of whom were old enough to remember the Saint when he served their father, received him, and with them the Saint probably arranged for his own release, and may have purchased the freedom of several of the Christian slaves they still held. Some of these he may have brought with him to Saul, others he may have sent back to their own Country.

For a number of years, the Saint confined his efforts to the North, presumably being confident of the ability of the companions he had left in Wicklow, to carry out the work there. With them, however, he kept in touch.

As the number of his converts increased, he erected

small wooden Churches, where the size of a congregation justified it and placed one of his companions in charge of each district.

In the midst of his labours, he trained young men for the priesthood, and instructed newly made Christians.

Extending his efforts into west of the country, to where he drove in his Chariot, the Saint made many converts during his sojourn in the quarter, after which he revisited the South, and established a number of Churches there. He also crossed the Irish Sea.

With the progress of his mission, came increasing opposition to his teaching. The poor had sympathetic ears. The walled-in Chieftains were antagonistic. Pagans and Pelagains attacked him. A sin of his early boyhood was awakened and hurled against him. He was accused of presumption; he was called unlearned. He was charged with unworthy motives. At his sermons he was repeatedly challenged.

With the meekness of his Divine Master, he met his opponents. Saint Patrick was no Druid, as many writers would have us believe. What though his opponents clamoured for him to make storms or rain, or walk-through fire? What though they called upon him to melt the snow? The gentle Patrick did not need to do such work, no, to even banish snakes from a land, where such reptiles could not live, in order to convince the Irish of his love of God and the truth of his teaching. He was a plain, straight-forward man who had no recourse to fantastic acts.

By the conversion of a thousand pagans, he worked a thousand miracles, and the greatest of all his miracles was the bringing of the Irish Nation to the Faith. At no time did he sail under false colours.

When he was being criticised by the learned, he never hesitated to proclaim, "I am in many respects imperfect," but he was not without the all-important knowledge for his mission, for he added: "yet I am not ignorant of the testimony of my Lord". How the proud Druids must have been confounded by this modest man, who, in answer to "The Voice of the Irish," that voice which had pleaded from the woods of Antrim: "We entreat thee, holy youth, that you come and henceforth walk amongst us", had come and was walking amongst them. His Bishopric, however, was not a bed of roses.

Over the long roads and the high hills, he and his priests had to travel. It was an arduous task that he had undertaken in a foreign country, and he was often homesick. So frequently did he speak, in his separation from parents, friends and country, that pain of exile seems to have become part of his teaching and been imparted to the Irish.

That he had left "forever", "his country and parents and many gifts which were offered, with weeping and tears," is what he tells us. His parents had been against him coming to Ireland. They could not forget the harm the Irish had once wrought upon their home and family. Even some of his seniors, in Gaul, had urged him not to go, while others called him a fool for going to such a wild country. But says: "It was not my grace but God who conquered in me and resisted them all, so that I came to the Irish people to preach the Gospel".

Offending his parents and friends, leaving home and country forever, he came to suffer, "insults from unbelievers" and endure reproaches "about his wanderings".

In the course of his travels throughout Ireland and Scotland, he met with many disappointments and had as he himself tells us, to "endure many persecutions" being tortured "even to chains". But the Saint persevered. Daily he "fished well and diligently" and as the Lord commanded him, continued "spreading his nets, so that a copious multitude and crowd might be taken". From the writings of the Saint, we are not able to trace the exact places that he visited, but tradition is marked heavy with his footsteps. That he founded many Churches. That he was abused by Kings and Chieftains. That he visited Scotland, Wales, and Isle of Man. That he braved and debated with the Druids. That he denounced the laws. That he made many priests. That he ordained several Bishops. That he baptised thousands of converts and that he founded Armagh, there appears no doubt. To accomplish all this, he spent many years in these countries, and as an old authority puts it, "was more than ordinary man".

With such humble beginnings as a barn at Saul, and in spite of tremendous and incessant opposition, this was a great accomplishment for a man no longer young. Small little Churches, erected by the willing hands of Christian workers, had sprung up in various places throughout Ireland and Scotland. The light of Armagh had dawned and was slowly spreading. The humble folk had given of their strength to build the House of God, and those, more favoured with riches, then followed to receive the Faith, for Saint Patrick tells us of "religious women who have given to me small voluntary gifts" to aid in the upkeep of the Churches.

As we have already learned, the Irish were fond of wearing ornaments, and it must have been an impressive sight in those early days, to behold, after one of Saint Patrick's sermons, ladies of the land walk up to the Alter, and removing their pagan jewellery, and place it there as an offering.

Here is how the Saint describes this himself: "And religious women have cast off their ornaments upon the Altar". These, he adds, he "used to return to them, but the donors were offended" at him for doing so.

Thus after some years, was Saint Patrick so encouraged and assisted by his converts in his good work, until he could eventually ask with gratitude "Whence then, has it come to pass that in Ireland, they, who never had any knowledge of God, and until now have always worshipped idols and unclean things, have lately become a people of the Lord and are called the sons of God, of whom sons and daughters of Chieftains, are seen to be monks and virgins of Christ". With this progress came the charge of selfish motives against the Saint.

By his enemies he was accused of being mercenary, but he had not come to Ireland to gather wealth. On the contrary, he came with much as we know and spent it freely in the service of God.

Denying himself many things, he replied to these critics: "I keep myself prudently in everything" and he tells us, he lived this so that he "might not give the unbelievers any occasion to defame or depreciate".

So particular we he, to serve the people without monetary reward, that in his Confession he pointedly alludes to having "baptised many thousand men" and not receiving a screpall (about three pence) and also to having ordained the many clergy "gratuitously". "If," he proclaims, "I asked any of them even the price of a shoe, tell it against me and I will restore you more."

From the Confession of the Saint, we learn many things. From it we know that he travelled "amid many perils, even to remote places where there was no one beyond, and where no one else had ever penetrated" and also that, as his flock increased, went from place to place "to baptise, convert, ordain clergy, or to confirm the people". And these duties, he tells us, "The Lord granting, I diligently and most cheerfully for your salvation, defrayed all things". How he and those saintly Christians were robbed in Ireland and Scotland, we can detect also from the Saint's writings. "During this time, I gave presents to Kings", he says, who unless he had done so, would not have permitted him to pass through their territory. To the pagan Kings, ehe generous Christian Missioners were excellent subjects for plunder.

Not satisfied with having received presents from Saint Patrick, for small favours, they even sent members of their families to accompany and impose upon him, and of these he writes: "I have pay to their sons who escorted me".

Even when in such company he was not free from molestation, for we learn that he was set upon and beaten. "They seized me together with my companions" he tells us, "And on that day they eagerly desired to kill me". We know not whether his assailants were "learned Druids" or King's servants, but we suspect that they were the latter. None of the members of the poorer classes in those days, could or would have dared to seize the Saint in company of King's children. "They bound me in iron," he states, and as well as being robbed of his valuables, he was imprisoned for fourteen days, evidently at the command of the mighty pagan King.

Only by a miracle was the Saint saved on this occasion, for he relates that: "the Lord set me free from their power". But the Kings and their sons were not the only imposters the Saint had to face. Like some of the modern American judges, the judges of those days had to receive presents for privileges and were not above imposing fines where they thought they could collect them. Of these gentlemen, the Saint says: "But you know how much I paid to those who acted as judges, throughout all the regions which I more frequently visited". He further adds: "For I think I distributed among them, not less than the hire of fifteen men (for a lifetime)".

But, as if proud of the sacrifice, the Saint concludes by saying: "I still spend and will spend myself for your souls". His heart was beating to a worthier ideal than that of riches. "Poverty and calamity suit me better than riches and luxuries" he avows; poverty and calamity the SLAVE-SAINT met amongst the Irish.

Such was Saint Patrick, the lover of poverty and the friend to the poor of Ireland.

The Epistle to Coroticus

In the last Chapter we examined briefly the Confession of Saint Patrick. In this chapter, we shall try to examine his Epistle to Coroticus.

When the Saint had been some time in Ireland as Bishop, he went from one district to another conferring the Sacraments. One Sunday he paid such a visit to some place where many converts had been received. The day following was a day of prayer and devotion.

All those who had received the sacraments had gathered and were thus engaged, when a band of brutal men rushed down upon the kneeling people, and killing several, carried off a large number of the girls. This happened in Ireland.

The name of the director of this expedition was Coroticus. Who and what he was we do not know, but how his men could rush into Ireland, do what they succeeded in doing, and then make off without interference, requires some explaining. Various writers have expressed different opinions regarding this leader, some contending that he was a Welsh Chieftain, called Caredig, some say that he was a Scotch ruler, called Ceretic and others that he was Carausius, who rebelled against the Roman Empire. Be who he may, Saint Patrick, immediately he heard of the outrage on his converts, wrote a letter to him, and from it we can form some idea of the awful difficulties of the first Bishop of the Irish.

That Coroticus had Irish warriors under his command is evident from his letter, so that one wonders if the Kings and Chieftains of Ireland, who have been made to appear such friends of Saint Patrick, were asleep when their land was invaded, their citizens slain, and others taken captive. Indeed, there is much in this incident that points deliberately to Kingly connivance.

Coroticus's warriors, they tell us, came down upon

these Christians, to obtain plunder, to secure slaves and to kill, and succeed well but they left behind them the bleeding bodies of Ireland's first Christian Martyrs.

The Epistle, or letter of protest that Saint Patrick wrote, was addressed to this man and in it he tells how his newly baptised were earnestly engaged in prayer, with the sign of the Cross still fresh upon their brows, when the wild raiders fell upon them, putting some to the sword and carrying others to captivity. This letter the Saint entrusted to a holy presbyter whom he informs us he had "taught from his infancy" and sent other clergy with him to endeavour to recover the "baptised captives whom they took", by pleading to the leaders. "But" he tells us, "They mocked at them."

This murderous onslaught about which he so strongly protested, is best described by the Saint himself. Here is what he said: "on the day after that, on which (these Christians) were anointed neophytes in white robes, and while the chrism was yet glistening on their foreheads, they were cruelly massacred and slaughtered with the sword."

This occurred at the time when the Saint had made considerable progress, for he tells us: "Since in these last times in Ireland has been most excellently and auspiciously planted and instructed by the favour of God." Even then, when he must have been a very old man, the patient Bishop and his flock encountered with

murderous opposition. In agony, he appealed to
Coroticus for the return of those Christian captives and
referring to his own self-sacrifice pathetically said: "Do
I not love pious compassion because I act (thus)
towards the nation which once took me captive and laid
waste the servants and handmaidens of my father's
house?". Then broken-heartedly, he cries out: "What
shall I do, Oh Lord? I am greatly despised. Behold thy
sheep are torn around me. Ravening wolves have
swallowed up the Flocks of the Lord". Then he makes
known to his attackers how much he has progressed
with the Salvation of the Irish, and states that his fold
"in Ireland was increasing with the greatest diligence
and the sons of the Irish and daughters of Princes, are
monks and virgins of Christ (In number) I cannot
enumerate". How different a story from that of the far-
off days when he was greeted on the banks of
Strangford Lough by a few fearing poorly clad
fishermen!

To Coroticus, Saint Patrick would seem to say: "I have
come to free slaves, you to make slaves", for he accuses
him of arranging to "sell them to foreign nation that
knows not God". Appealing for such, he writes:
"wherefore, the Church laments and bewails her sons
and daughters whom the sword has not yet slain, but
who have been carried to distant parts and exported into
far-off lands where sin manifestly is shamelessly
stronger". To all this Coroticus, like the Irish Kings and

Chieftains closed his ears and heart. What did he or his followers care for the poor unarmed barefoot Christian Bishop, who so foolishly gave away all his worldly goods in the service of God's poor.

As if in despair, the tortured Saint deplores: "Therefore with sadness and sorrow I will cry out, O my most beautiful and most beloved brethren and sons whom I begot in Christ – I cannot count you – what shall I do for you? I am not worthy before God and men to help". Prostrate with grief at the awful calamity, he finds consolation in the thought that his baptised one have passed to their eternal reward, and says, "Thanks be to God, baptised believers, ye have passed from this world to paradise".

"Thanks be to God," is what Saint Patrick said almost 1,500 years ago. How often do we hear this today in Ireland?

The Death of Saint Patrick

Had the writing of the first Lives of Saint Patrick not been so long delayed, much less confusion regarding him would have existed today.

About the time and place of his birth, the duration and location of his captivity, the place of his teaching, the length of his life etc., there have been many opinions. And so, the same difficulty arises in respect to his death.

I have endeavoured to p rove to you that Palladius and Patrick were the same person and I have no patience with the frantic foolish efforts to efface Palladius. In trying to discover how Saint Patrick died, we must keep before us the fact that he was also known as Palladius.

The first Life of Saint Patrick was not written, as already pointed out, for over two hundred years after his death. Apart, therefore, from the two documents written by Saint Patrick himself and the entries in Prosper's Chronicle in regard to Palladius, most of the stories of the Saint had passed from mouth to mouth, and no doubt grew in the passing over such a very long period. To put implicit faith in them would be neither reasonable nor honest.

The reference of Prosper, regarding one Palladius being obtainable. The old Latin documents being signed Patricius and tradition being much confused in respect to both these names, the inevitable result was an effort, by the first historians, to separate them. Thus began the legend and, we might say, muddle of Saint Patrick, one sheep having jumped over the gate, all others followed.

Why the first two Bishops who concerned themselves about the writing of the Life of the Saint, and who accepted that Palladius came first, did not undertake the life of the latter instead, is difficult to understand. Had they written of Palladius, the mystery might have long since been solved or never arisen. Certainly, it would have been much better for future history if they had done so.

The old scribes being only given the task of recording Saint Patrick, and having his writings before them, had to make incidents tally, and in ticking off this, against that, he had to be brought to Ireland in the year 432, but as there was no getting past the fact that Palladius had arrived in 431, the latter had to be bundled out of the way, as quickly as possible. So as to make room for their Patrick, thus riding over Irish and Scottish traditions.

Scottish Tradition, fortunately, was not to be so easily ignored, and has been much more kind to the memory of Palladius, so that when we want to learn anything about him, we much go to Scottish records.

Ireland strove to forget him, yet was unable, in face of fact, to dispute his coming as first Bishop to the Irish in 431.

For other Irish Saints, historians found excuses for change of names, but not so with Palladius, who undoubtedly did become known in his day as Patrick. Having once decided that they were two different Bishops, childish efforts were made to make every detail about them different.

Palladius came from Gaul, so Patrick had to come from somewhere else. Patrick, having been a slave in Ireland, knew Irish so Palladius did not know the language. Palladius came to fight Pelagianism, so Patrick came to convert pagans only. Palladius left Ireland and never returned, so Patrick came to Ireland and never left. Palladius died soon, so Patrick had to live long. Palladius had been in Scotland and England, so Patrick was not permitted to visit either. But in spite of these innumerable other divisions, few historians could get past the fact both had been with Germanus of Auxerre, and on his instructions, it was generally accepted, were sent to the Irish.

With the repeated confusion that arose in respect to the various happenings in the Life of Saint Patrick on account of the two names, it is but natural that a similar lack of agreement should have arisen in respect to his death.

When the Saint was a slave, he prayed continually to be free, and his prayer was answered. When he returned home, he prayed that he might become a deacon and God also answered that prayer. When a deacon, he asked his Divine Master to send him to teach the Irish, and he was made a Bishop and despatched. When in Ireland, he prayed continually for its conversion, and we know how his prayer was heard. In his own writings we discover that he also prayed to become a martyr to the Faith, so let us see if this prayer of Saint Patrick was eventually answered.

Out of his own record we are able to note how terrible was the persecution and punishment he endured at the hands of Irish people. Palladius, who was supposed to precede him and to have died before he arrived and whose grave Saint Patrick is said to have come North to visit, is never mentioned once by him. Yet the Saint was just such a man to have immortalised Palladius, if this had really happened.

Some writers have been at pains to try and prove that the Saint made himself a Bishop, without realising that, in his Confession, he makes such an assertion appear absurd, by saying of himself: "Behold thou art to be promoted to the Rank of Bishop". From being the deacon, Palladius, he was therefore promoted to be Bishop of the Irish and came back to Ireland in the year 431. We know how brutally he had been treated by the Irish in his boyhood. We know how they had wrecked his home, abused his father's servants, took him captive, held him in slavery for years, and how in spite of all this and in spite of the tears of his parents and protestations of his friends, he came back to Christianize the nation that had thus treated him. Back, as he says himself, to endure "many snares" and to encounter "things which I cannot express in words".

What, we might well ask, were these things which the saintly man could not "express in words". From several quarters, his opposition came and came continually and increasingly, throughout his long years of zealous missionary work. Many, he tells us, hindered his mission, men denounced him as a slave, can we not discern the spirit of Saint Patrick's teaching? Everywhere he wandered throughout Ireland, Scotland, and Wales, he was met with hostility and insults. About all this, there is no doubt whatever, as he tells us of it himself. Kings, Chieftains, and men of learning enraged the people against him and organised opposition continually. Missiles were thrown at him on his journeys, and at his religious ceremonies.

Permission to travel by certain routes were denied him. In other parts he had to pay heavily to enter the areas. His charioteer was killed by an arrow, that was meant for the Saint himself. But Saint Patrick was a brave man – a man who feared not to die for the Faith that was in him, and much of this courage he had imparted to the Irish, who eventually embraced his teaching. No amount of opposition could daunt him. Manfully he persevered and even dared his attackers to do their worst. The sneers, abuse and onslaughts seen to have only made him more determined and with a supreme Christian resignation, he battled on. But his enemies were numerous, and they meant to kill him, as we know from the Saint himself, that they made at least twelve serious attacks upon his life. At no time does he appear to have been free from danger. Even when his mission was almost at an end, and his long days of untiring service to the Irish were nearly finished, he was not immune from injury. As an old, beleaguered servant of God, he writes in his Confession: "because I daily expect either murder, or to be circumvented or reduced to slavery, or mishap of some kind". Then in that courageous old age, we can understand something of the heart of the Saint, for he says: "But I fear none of these things".

Dichu, Saint Patrick's friend and guardian was dead. No protection that he could now command, however, how sufficient to save him. Even when he actually, paid the sons of Kings to guard him through their own friend's territory, he was robbed, taken prisoner and held in chains for fourteen days. Only the Lord, he tells us, saved his life on that occasion. Again, had the prayer of this Saintly old warrior been heard. Of one occasion we know, (and there may have been many others) where his followers were attacked at prayer, where a service was broken up, and where a large number of the congregation were brutally murdered, and many carried off. This happened in Ireland, and efforts are repeatedly made to induce us to believe that the barbarous outrage was only committed by foreigners. It is difficult to accept. After the slaying of his converts, as the Saint wept over the torn bodies of his slaughtered, innocent children, he solemnly prayed: "I pray Him to grant me that with those proselytes and captives I may pour out my blood for His name's sake, even although I myself may even be deprived of burial

and my corpse most miserably be torn limb from limb
by dogs or wild beasts, or that the fowls of heaven
should devour it". Thus did Saint Patrick implore his
God, and as his prayers were so frequently answered on
other occasions, one naturally wonders if this request
were also answered.

To it having been granted, there is much that points, in
which the silence of Ireland in respect to its Saint for
over two hundred years, is not the least.

That he should become a martyr for the Faith was
undoubtedly the earnest desire of the Saint. He lived in
the age of martyrs. He invited the supreme sacrifice.
Numbers of his flock were slain. He prayed to share
their fate, and that he "poured out his blood for his
name's sake" at the hands of those to whom he came to
bring the Faith, is difficult to deny. Does not the strange
silence of the Irish, that lasted for so long after his
death, point to nation's guilt? To Coroticus he had said:
"I dwelt thus among barbarians" and admonished him
severely for his brutality, but Coroticus scoffed at him,
and later he and his men may have taken part in the
murdering of the Saint himself.

Let us try to examine carefully a few of the various
records that may have any useful bearing upon his
death. Many dates have been offered for it, and many
places. William of Malmesbury, says, it occurred in the
year 472 and that he was buried in the Old Church of

Glastonbury. The Annals of Ulster state 492 as the year. The Annals of the Four Masters give 493, and more modern writers plump for 461, while several say he died in an earlier century altogether.

This confusion, as I have pointed out, exists in respect to almost everything connected with the Saint, but we do know for certain, and there is no escaping from it, that on Palladius, as a Bishop came to Ireland in the year 431, and the Scotch, who in those days were but part of the Irish, insist that he stayed a long time in these islands. Tradition is overwhelming against his being hurried away. Baronius, a Roman Annalist, admits that the Irish received their first Bishop from Pope Celestine, and the Venerable Bede, in later years, stated that "Palladius was sent to the Scots (Irish) as their first Bishop by Pope Celestine". Pope Celestine sent Palladius to "the Scots believing in Christ" that is, to the Irish in Ireland, Scotland, Wales etc., and not merely to the Irish in Ireland. Palladius, therefore, having come to introduce a prelatical form of government among these countries, he was expressly "their first Bishop".

According to Buchanan, he was the very first to set up Bishops in Scotland, where, up to the time of his coming, there had been no Bishops whatsoever. Then Boethius tells us that Palladius "was the first that exercised holy magistracy (prelacy) among the Scots, being by the Pope created Bishop", While Johannes

Major States: "Before Palladius, the Scotch were nourished in the Faith by Presbyters and Monks, without Bishops".

Palladius then was first Bishop of all the Scots (Irish) in all their colonies. He came to his Bishopric and did not die soon after, but continued to make history even in Scotland, by founding Churches, baptising converts, consecrating bishops, and also converting Servanus and Tervanus. With this progress in that country, he is tenaciously linked, and no one doubts that all his work took place at exactly the same time as Saint Patrick was said to be Bishop of the Irish. How, therefore, could they have been different?

And now to return to the death of our Saint. We have said that he and Palladius were one and the same. On reaching Ireland both at least were credited with having received rough handling. Palladius, they tell us, was chased and Patrick beaten. Several of those historians who have endeavoured to prove that Saint Patrick did not recognised Rome, inform us that Palladius was chased because he came from the Pope, and forget the opposition that Saint Patrick informs us he received. No matter how comfortable it may have been for some to presume that Saint Patrick did not preach in Scotland, every fact stubbornly arrays itself against this. Saint Patrick followed his flock. He visited Scotland and made priests and bishops in Scotland. To the name Palladius which early Scotch historians had read in

Prosper, is attached all his work in that country.

Almost every ancient writer, as well as tradition, point to Palladius like Patrick having met with tremendous hostility during his mission and his death would appear to have been in perfect keeping with the prayer of Patrick – who daily expected to be killed. In Saint Patrick's Epistle to Coroticus, written about the middle of his mission, it says: "I am despised by some" but near the end of his life when he came to write his Confession, he said: "I am despised by most". Would this difference not convince us that the opposition he was meeting with had grown infinitely stronger and more dangerous, and that he expected anything to happen?

In respect to Saint Patrick's passing, the Irish historians have been exceptionally charitable, and have given him a peaceful death, and found him a quiet grave with saintly company. To Palladius the Scotch were almost equally kind. Yet I do not believe there is a single serious historian who is not convinced that one of them was murdered.

Most Irish historians have said it was Palladius, but the Scotch writers did not retaliate, by saying it was Patrick. Rather they merely contented themselves by saying that their Bishop Palladius lived a long time and passed away peacefully.

About the place of Palladius's death. There are two

readings in the manuscript of Muirchu, "in Britonum finibus" and "in Pictorum finibus" and it merely says, "he died". To the copy of Tirechan, a paragraph, added probably by the scribe Ferdomnach, states: "Palladius suffered martyrdom among the Scots". The Tripartite Life says: "Sickness seized him in Scotland" and he died there. Others say he died in Ulster, and that Saint Patrick came to that province for this reason. A careful examination of the earliest written lives exposes what would seem to be a deliberate reluctance to accept Palladius as Patrick.

As well as the paragraph in Tirechan, many subsequent writers have agreed he was "martyred amongst the Scots" and by some Irish historians the country of the Picts (Scotland) is pointed out as his burial place, the exact spot being given by them as Fordun, where in the year 1494 his supposed relics were disinterred there and placed in a silver shrine by Archbishop William Schewes of St. Andrew, to later disappear.

As you will have seen from the foregoing, most Irish writers did not like to admit that Palladius had been martyred in Ireland, whilst the earliest historians strove to make Patrick a kind of independent Bishop to fit the radical pride.

Palladius being Patrick, and as Palladius was martyred, we are forced to the conclusion that Saint Patrick was murdered and was murdered by the Irish. Almost every historic fact and tradition go to strengthen the belief that he became a martyr and that his prayer was answered.

Where he was slain, we do not know for certain, but we realise that behind the suggestion, that when Saint Patrick came as Bishop to Ireland, he was supposed to go North to visit a Martyr's grave, there may be some guidance.

When we recall that the Life of the Saint was not written until over two hundred years after his death, and that the people then living in the North of Ireland, believed a grave of some Martyred Bishop to have been in their territory, would this not point to the presence of his remains? Even in the Southern Counties, it was generally recognised that a Roman Bishop had arrived there in 431, went North and was martyred. This Bishop could have been none other than Saint Patrick. Do not forget that Christianity did not find its way suddenly over the whole of Ireland. At large the people remained heathen for some time after Saint Patrick had died. The Kings did not obey his call, and for many years after, were more than half pagan. To the Druids they clung strongly, and with them, continued to resist the new Faith for years. Curses had been showered upon the Christian Bishop, who had come to brave these powerful Druids, but for a time he survived. Then efforts were made to slay him, efforts that continued, until they became frequent, and eventually succeeded.

Saint Patrick was slain, and his followers trembled. The Druids in the meantime had won. The Martyr's companions, the Martyr's followers, the gentle early

Druids

Christians were silenced. Then came a period when the Christian religion was almost entirely destroyed, both in Ireland and Scotland. Many Christians were slaughtered, and Saint Patrick himself was almost forgotten. The Kings and Druids would not hear of his name, but towards a sacred spot somewhere in the North, the trembling fingers of the early Irish Christians used to point.

In the North, Saint Patrick had been enslaved. In the North he settled. In the North he was imprisoned. In the North his converts were slaughtered. In the North he founded Armagh. In the North he wrote the Confession in which he made it perfectly clear, that he expected to be murdered at any moment, and this, he signed beneath the tragic statement: "This is my Confession before I die".

When, after hundreds of years had passed away, and Southern Irish historians had taken up the task of recording his life, they were confronted with the unconquerable Southern tradition that a Roman Bishop, who had once called at Wicklow, "sailed North" and "was martyred there".

In the South, tradition had it thus, while, in the North it pointed to his place of burial there. Thus, being faced by the names of Palladius and Patrick, and unable, or unwilling to discern in both Saint Patrick, one had to die soon and the other live long. Palladius therefore, was said to have been martyred, and the Irish made to have been kind to Saint Patrick, thus accounting for the neglect, in respect to this grave (Palladius) for over seven hundred years.

Not until the year 1186, do we hear much of this, the sacred resting place of Ireland's martyred Bishop. John DeCourcey was then in the country, and the lands of

Ulster were red with blood. In the midst of all the slaughter and destruction, the devout peasants of the County of Down cherished a devotion that had been handed down through the generations for a little hill overlooking the present town of Downpatrick. There they believed the remains of the martyred Saint rested.

St. Patricks Grave in Downpatick

DeCourcey was not long in the country, when he learned of this, and every effort was made to discover the exact spot. Prayers were offered up by pious people, that it might be found. On a certain night, a light was said to have been seen above a certain spot in the old Church then there. The floor was dug up, and the bones of three bodies were found. These, it was decided, were the remains of Saint Patrick, Saint Brigid and Saint Columcille. Messengers were dispatched post haste to

Rome, and in due course the solemnities of translation were conducted. The bones were placed in separate coffins and again put underground. This spot, today, is covered by a huge stone on which is inscribed the name Patric and is to be seen near the Cathedral of Downpatrick.

If John DeCourcey had had less to do with this discovery, we might be disposed to accept the remains, without demur. Furthermore, profound students of Columcille are not impressed that their Saint reposes there. In addition to this, we have the strange opinion expressed by Cardinal Baronius, regarding Vivian, who co-operated largely with DeCourcey, in respect to discovery.

At least we are satisfied that the hill in question is where our Saint was buried. In the minds of the people, we discover his grave. For over seven hundred years that little mound, on which now rests the inscribed stone, had been a place of prayer. A martyred Christian Bishop, tradition told, was buried there. It was the grave of Saint Patrick, the first Christian Bishop of the Scots (Irish) who "suffered martyrdom" at their hands. It was the grave that Bishop Tirechan must have known of, about the year 700. It was the grave the early Christians, often spoke of and must have visited. It was the outstanding grave in Ireland, when DeCourcey came.

There is a paragraph in Bishop Tirechan's Life of Saint Patrick, that we must not overlook, when we come to enquire how Saint Patrick died. It is short, but it speaks volumes, and to the reader anxious for the truth, should leave no doubt. Remember it is contained in one of the earliest Lives written and is the record of a holy man. Here it is: "Palladius, the Bishop, is first sent, who by another name is called Patrick, who suffered martyrdom among the Scots (of Ireland), as ancient Saints relate".

Mark you, he says: "as ancient Saints relate". In other words, he has supported the statement that Palladius was called Patrick, and was martyred in Ireland, by informing us that he had reliable grounds for this record. Either, he had been told of this by holy men long since dead or had read it from some saintly writings. Nothing, I think could be clearer, nor more convincing than this statement in Bishop Tirechan's Life. It points conclusively to the fact that Palladius was Patrick, and that Patrick was murdered by those he had come to save, and that "ancient Saints" believed this also.

Thus was the prayer of Ireland's Patron Saint answered. Thus, had he become a Martyr, that by his years of suffering and agony of death, he might save the souls of the Irish.

St. Patrick's Connection to Belfast

This a reprint of an article Cahal Bradley authored in 1952 for golden jubilee of Holy Cross Church located in Cahal's home, Ardoyne, Belfast.

Did St. Patrick Come This Way?

Belfast Lough

In writing of the district above Belfast to which the first of the Passionist Fathers came in the year 1868 it is necessary to begin as far back as the time of our National Apostle, Saint Patrick. The Saint, in his Confession, tells us that when he was a mere boy, he was taken by marauding warriors from his home and with many others carried off to captivity in Ireland. It was to the County Antrim Chieftain Milcho, he and presumably other victims, were sold into slavery and as the territory of this chieftain skirted the waters we know as Belfast Lough, it is natural to assume the boatmen brought the captives that way. The very first view the boy Patrick had of Ireland, therefore, must have been of the shores of Antrim and Down and it is reasonable to conclude that the first time the put his foot on Irish soil it was on the Antrim Shore and as the boats of those years came to the sands and deep into the Lough for safety. The prisoners would have been landed on the white sands of the White Ford at the junction of the River Lagan, the Lough, and the River Farset. That spot, which should have some memorial to mark it, would not have been far from where the Albert Clock now sands in Belfast.

River Facet – Note Albert Clock in background.

Junction of the River Lagan, the Lough, and the River Farset – where Patrick is believed to have first landed in Ireland.

Up the Shankill from the Sea

From nearby one of the oldest of the known highways
of those days existed. For many centuries later it bore
the name of The Old Church Road. Today, that part of
it passing through the City of Belfast is called the
Shankill (Old Church) Road. This was the highway that
led over the mountains to the stronghold of the Antrim

Holy Cross Church Ardoyne, Belfast

Chieftain Milcho and by this route the boy Patrick
would have travelled, thus, passing along where now is
the Woodvale Road and by the very spot where the
Passionist Fathers have today their monastery and
beautiful church on his way to the Parish of The Braid
and to his serfdom on the Hill of Slemish. There he tells
us he had to look after cattle. For six long years he was
employed night and day as a Shepherd. In those times it

was the custom to move the herds to fresh pastures and as the lands of Milcho embraced the hills above Belfast, which Patrick could have seen from Slemish, the young slave-boy, during his years of captivity, may have also herded his master's flocks on the very slopes where now stands the Church of Holy Cross.

Patrick's Escaper Route and Missionary Path

After this period of time St Patrick tells us he "took to flight". In making his escape he would have travelled along the road that led south from The Braid district. This would have been the same road that he had tramped to captivity and would have brought him over the hills, across where is now the Horseshoe, down what we know as Goat's Loaney, through Ardoyne Loaney and on via the Old Church (Shankill) Road to the White Ford in order to cross the Lagan there at low tide and pursue his journey south to the port from which he sailed to freedom. Again, he would have passed by what we, today, call Ardoyne Corner.

Cottages on Ardoyne Corner

When the years went by and the boy Patrick came back to Ireland as a Christian Missioner to be received by the men of the Sea around Strangford Lough, which became his Irish Sea of Galilee, we learn that soon after his first Church had been established at Saul, in County Down, he left his boats in the charge of Chieftain Dichu and proceeded to visit his old master Milcho in order to secure his freedom and to himself the right to do his missionary work in the territory. To make this journey he would travel by the old Rathkelter highway and thence by the Old Church (Shankill) Road, on past Ardoyne and over the hills as he had done as a boy.

The White Church of St. Patrick

As subsequent events would go to prove no better welcome was accorded to Our Saint anywhere than that which he received on the shores and neighborhood of Belfast Lough. Here he must have taken an exceptionally warm interest in the locality and people. Immediately after Down he and his friends must have

Baptismal Font from St. Mathews Church Belfast

concentrated on the area now covered by the city of Belfast which, as you will understand, was not unknown to him. Indeed, the Monasticon Hibernicum offers support to the strong tradition by stating, "St. Darerca, Sister of St Patrick was Abbess of a nunnery on the spacious plain along the River Lagan". This nunnery is taken to have been at Frian's Bush (Stranmillis) so that St Patrick had his sister to keep him in his work.

129

On what is known now as the Shankill Road, and not far from Tennent Street, the parent Church of the area was built. All authorities believe it to have been erected in the fifth century. For many hundreds of years, it and its other five chapels flourished. The name, it carried down the centuries and is still remembered by, is the White Church of St Patrick. This sacred site, which was in the Ancient Parish of Shankill, is not far from

St. Matthews Church – Note Shamrock Design

Ardoyne and is now in the Holy Cross Father's District. Only a large stone Baptismal font remains of St Patrick's historic White Church, and this is to be seen on the Woodvale Road near Cambrai Street.

Shankill Graveyard – believed to be 1500 years old.

From that beginning other Churches sprang up. At the foot of High Street, by the side of the river Farsett, the Chapel of Saint Patrick of White Ford stood for many centuries, as did others in the Ancient Parish. In many early documents the names of Shankill and its churches appear. The taxation of Pope Nicholas of March 1291 describes the White Church as Ecclesia Alba cum Capella de Vado and the later record known as the Pope's Terrier of 1613 also mentions it. In both of these the Churches of Kilpatrick, Cranoge, Killeror Callender's Fort, Crookmock etc., are given as in the Parish of Shankill and under the care of the White Church of St Patrick.

From this fifth century development came the spread of the faith along the shores of Belfast Lough and the rising of the great monastic of Bangor, Holywood, White Abbey, Carnmoney etc. preceding the glorious golden centuries when Ireland won for herself the title of the Isle of Saints and Scholars. To the securing of that honour no parish made a greater contribution than the old historic Parish of Shankill.

When the Passionists Came

In his Ecclesiastical Antiquities, Church of Ireland Bishop, Dr. William Reeves (1815 -1892) says, "At the time of the Reformation the parish of Shankill contained six Chapels," so that as early as the fifth century and also in the sixteenth century this grand old Parish with its Chapels flourished under the patronage and protection of the Irish Chieftains. Then, in the year 1604, came the plantation of Ulster followed by the flight of the Earls and intense persecution of a people left unprotected and disheartened. From a document dated April 1621, giving a description of the district in that year, we can form some idea of the destruction that was wrought. The Tuagh, or district, is described as embracing Whitehouse, Hyde Park, Ligoniel and extending to the Lagan. Ruins of ancient Churches and ruins of many homes fill the record. Sir Arthur Chichester had written to his King that, "He would rather labour with his hands in the plantation of Ulster than dance and play in that of Virginia."

Always a menace to invaders, the mountains overlooking the town of Belfast were attacked and swept clean of all their habitations. Naturally the hills of Ligoniel (O'Neill's Hollow) where the men of O'Ncill camped, and from where they after attacked, received the most ruthless attention.

Describing one of his journeys, Chichester says – "I

burned – sparing none of what quality, age or sex, soever, besides many burned to death, we kill man, woman and child, horse, beast and whatsoever we find." No wonder this "fayre Tuagh" had speedily become barren and appeared in the inquisition of 1621 as a place of ruins and devastation. Their homes destroyed, their lands taken from them, any frantic resistance offered by the dispossessed people was blazoned as acts of highwaymen and freebooters. Stories of the brothers O'Haughan (c 1717) and their exploits still abound in the old parish and the places of their hiding and holding-up are frequently pointed out.

For many years the slopes and hills to the North of Belfast became a wilderness topped by the Hill of Wolves, now known as Wolfhill, and it was not until early in the last century that its complexion showed a change.

Holy Cross, Ardoyne, it is often said, has been the result of a mission. St Patrick and his Missioners had come from Strangford Lough to Shankill Parish in the fifth century and following in the Saint's footsteps the Passionist Fathers came from Strangford shore (Portaferry) to Ardoyne in the nineteenth century.

The years immediately before their coming had brought changes. For these, the growing demand for linen was mainly responsible. Bleaching machinery had already been introduced in other districts as early as 1725 but, although the swelling streams that travelled down the mountains may have attracted industrialists, the elevated wilderness and entire absence of suitable roads had prevented an early introduction of that kind of work. Bleaching however, was eventually established at Glenbank, and after, the linen mills followed in its wake.

Wolfhill and Ligoniel

Around and near these industrials' small workers' dwellings (on mill rows, as they were called) commenced to rise until, before the year 1850, two growing little villages known as Wolfhill and Ligoniel appeared on what had formerly been "a wilderness between the hills" and at Glenbank the picturesque little village bearing the lovely name of Harmony tried to hide itself in the trees by the side of the river. In these villages on the mountain, some Catholic families from various parts of Ireland, still hungry from the famine, found work and homes.

Above Wolfhill the River Forth comes tumbling down Ligoniel, Glenbank and on to Springfield. Along that two mile stretch more industries existed and were supplied by waterpower than on many a much larger and broader tract of water.

For a century hundreds of workers found employment and homes grew, for the River Forth was the And-na-crusha of Belfast in those days. It was the age of waterpower and many huge waterwheels in bright colours were to be seen whirling among the trees. The largest of these, and indeed the largest in Ulster, carried power to Emerson's Bleachworks. At Wolfhill another wheel of peculiar make sent out a tock-tock-tock kind of noise all day. At Ligoniel, Glenbank, Ferguson's Glen and near the Ballygomartin Road there were beetling establishments. Three of these and a Bleachworks were clustered together in the glen mentioned, and the remains of some of them can be seen today near Ewart's sports ground.

Above Ligoniel, is the hill of white lime quarries. This, in earlier times, was called the white mountain. Today it is known as Squires Hill and, because of the abundance of blaeberries that grow high up amongst its heather, is often referred to as blaeberry hill. As the town of Belfast grew so also grew the demand for the white stone. Homes required whitewash, bleachers required lime, boats required ballast, roads required surfacing and farmers required lime for their fields. Many men found work as quarrymen, Carters and homes appeared where none had been for hundreds of years.

Michael Andrews – Edenderry and Ardoyne

Much nearer the town and on the opposite side of the road to where the Passionists came, another industry had been started and a village had grown up beside it. Early in the nineteenth century, an enterprising young man called Michael Andrews, from County Down, had opened a business in Belfast and had secured a lease of a number of acres at this spot. Proceeding to establish a Hand-loom factory he reconstructed what few old homes were there and meeting with success in his business, gradually added more and more workers homes until eventually the quaint and busy little village, with its bell-tower and clock, its pebbled square, its bell-man calling out the hours at night, its snow white homes, its sturdy school, its quoit pitch and its loom-throbbing factory, became one of the leading attractions for people of the town. All these were there when the Fathers came to Ardoyne. Today they are no more.

Mr Andrews was the first to introduce the Jacquard Machine into Ireland. This gave a great impetus to his Factory and during the hundred years of its existence beautiful damask cloths were woven and supplied to King, Queen, Sultan, Maharajah, Dukes, President and to his holiness the Pope.

The home of this County Down man was situated at the back of where the Forum Picture House now stand. Almost hidden in its walled grounds by rows of large trees it had a gate-lodge on the front of the road almost opposite where the priests had their first monastery and where now is Holy Cross Hall and Schools. To this residence he gave a name they carried from his native country – the name 'Ardoyne House'.

It was in this way the name Ardoyne (John's Hill) came and took root in Edenderry, Belfast. To the townland this man's oft-applauded effort brought work and people and the first fathers found a warm welcome from parishioners in the little village of Ardoyne. Often, I have heard old residents say, that although officially there was no such a place as Ardoyne, Belfast, yet "any spot within the hearing of the monastery bell is Ardoyne".

From the Shankill to the Moon

The territory to which the Holy Fathers (as the Passionists were then affectionately called by the people) came in the summer of 1868 was very scattered. "From the Courthouse to the mountains and from the Shankill to the moon" was how some parishioners used to humorously describe it.

The linen mills had been developing and trade was increasing. At the back of Savages Mill, Savages Row, now Ardilea Street, had a large number of workers' homes. In Mitchell's Row, now Brookfield Street, and in the Cross Row, now Crumlin Street, it was the same. Almost all of these homes were occupied by Catholic families. From these and others, here and there, in the rapidly developing area the Fathers received an enthusiastic reception.

Although the parish in which they were to undertake their great work was large and scattered, they could not have failed but to have been both pleased and impressed by its wild and commanding beauty.

The Edenderry (Hill brow of the Oak grove) corner with its beautiful trees, its snug stone Point Cottage and garden, its green toll house, its old Manor and small white cottages and its background of the high Divis mountains must have looked well in the summer sun of 1868. Here they were to make their home and pursue their ministry.

What the Fathers Saw in August 1868

In those days, the white limestone from the White Mountain was used for surfacing the roads and the Crumlin, Shankill and Ligoniel roads were snowy white, so much so, that on strong sunny days, the glare from them irritated the eyes. By the many big, bright, red carts full of limestone that came bumping down from the mountain the faces of the roads were powdered daily by the white line that fell through their open joints.

Old residents remember Johnny's box which stood at the corner of the Woodvale, Crumlin Road. This was the toll house with its ground-weighbridge and its four funny little metal pillars in front. On this bridge the carts going to the town and returning were weighed and a toll collected on the tonnage. From there the white road to the mountains ran between touching trees, here and there skirted by white thorn, and, passing rows and rows of glistening white linen bleaching in the sun between there and the Big Green at Glenbank. Along what is now the Woodvale Road a few one-story, white-washed cottages were the only relief to the green fields and hedges that stretched to the Black Mountain. All these have since disappeared and the fields are covered, today, by the Woodvale estate.

On the Crumlin Road, above the mills, from Brookfield Street the line of ditches was only broken by a few houses while the plantation fields stretched on to the mountains in the rear . On the opposite side of the road, Quality Row (now Leopold Street) had only one side and nothing, but fields lay between it and the Woodvale Road. Where Butler Street, its adjoining streets and the Glenard district is today was a place of a few large farms and farmsteads where many cattle were grazed and where a lovely cane ran from the Village of Weavers to a little wooden bridge across the Rosehead River (a favourite bathing place of those days) and past the River Row of garden homes long since demolished.

Old Memories of Old Men

Often, from the older folk of Ardoyne, I have heard the story of the coming of the first Passionist Fathers to Belfast. From them I learned of the warm-hearted reception they received and, how after long hours of exacting labour in the mills, the workingmen of the district came with their saws, hatches and shovels each night to the hill above the town and there, worked until far into the morning, removing the many trees and preparing the ground to make a site for the first church. In co-operation with the men, the women of the district provided tea for the good priests and their helpers. While the building of the Church was proceeding these workmen also provided nightly protection in case of attacks which were frequently threatened.

The old Holy Cross Church facing Crumlin Road

To the erection of the first lovely Church on Edenderry Hill, these early Parishioners made a memorable contribution and no more impressive tribute could be paid to their work and the work of the first Priests than to record that in the short period of six months the building was complete and ready for opening.

In concluding, I would like to recall what was said many years ago by a devout old man who prided himself in being one of the first to have welcomed the Fathers to Ardoyne – "They came in Patrick's footsteps" he said, and he added, "They came to plant a Cross upon a hill above Belfast and they planted Holy Cross."

Opening of Holy Cross

NEW CHURCH,

OF

THE PASSIONIST FATHERS.

ARDOYNE, BELFAST

On SUNDAY 10th JANUARY. 1869.

HIGH MASS

Will commence at Twelve o'clock precisely, at which the Most Rev. Dr. Dorrian, Lord Bishop of the Diocese, will assist Pontifically.

After the Gospel, a Sermon will be preached by the Very Rev. F. Alphonsus O'Neill, Passionist, Superior of St. Paul's College. Dublin; after which there will be a Collection towards defraying the expenses of the New Church.

EVENING SERVICE

At Seven o'clock Vespers: Sermon by the Rev. F. Pius Devine, Professor of Theology, Passionists' College, Dublin, Litany of the Blessed Virgin and Benediction of the Blessed Sacraments Collection after the Sermon.

Admission by Tickets:—Morning Service—Reserved Seats, 5s.; Lower Seats, 2s. 6d. Evening Service—Reserved Seats, 2s. 6d.; Lower Seats, 1s.

N.B.—The number of Tickets will be issued in proportion to the number of persons the Church can accommodate; hence those who would favor us with their attendance are respectfully requested to apply for Tickets in time.

Tickets to be had at Mr. Owen Kerr's, Castle Place, Mr. Thomas Gribben's, 76 North Street; Mrs. McAuley's, Upper Arthur Street; Mr. McEntee's, Mill Street; and from the Passionist Fathers, Ardoyne, Belfast.

ABOUT THE AUTHOR

Born in 1886 in Belfast, Ireland, Cahal Bradley was a man of his times and an extraordinary one at that. A journalist,

Cahal (bottom right) his wife Mary, brothers Peter Francis (front left) and Hugh (top left)

businessman, published poet and novelist as well as an important Irish Nationalist politician. As a young man Cahal had mastered the Irish language through his participation the local Gaelic League. He was also a founder of a GAA club in Ardoyne that still

functions today. He was a contemporary of the great Irish Nationalist of his day such as Sean MacDermott and Blumer Hobson and like his father and brothers Cahal was a member of the Irish Republican Brotherhood. In 1920 he stood for and was elected to the office of deputy mayor of Derry as a

Derry Corp Council - Cahal front row third from left

Sinn Fein candidate and in later life was an Anti-Partition League Senator in the Northern Ireland Stormont government. He died in 1957 in his beloved Ardoyne.

NEXT STOP HEAVEN SERIES

READ ALL THE BOOKS IN THE SERIES!

Set in old Belfast, Cahal Bradley weaves a love story through the mill streets of the Bone, old Ardoyne and the roads up towards Ligoniel. It is a story of a young couple, Ned and Sheila, whose love for each other endures through poverty, violence and separation from each other when Sheila must immigrate to America.

Set in the period from 1905 through 1921 in Belfast, 'Next Stop Romance' follows the main character, Art O'Neill, from his first encounters with Irish Republicanism as a boy of fifteen, through the Irish War of Independence. Along the way Art finds himself in a plot to kidnap a famous actor as well as a village saving shootout with the Black and Tans, all while trying to carry on a romance.

COMING IN 2024!
CAHAL BRADLEY BOOK OF POEMS!!

Printed in Great Britain
by Amazon